CAROLINE HENNESSY & KRISTIN JENSEN

Sláinte

THE COMPLETE GUIDE

To IRISH

CRAFT BEER AND CIDER

NEW ISLAND

Praise for the book

'The resurgence of craft beers and ciders in Ireland has been one of the most exciting aspects of the real food revolution that is currently taking the country by storm. But it has arrived with astonishing speed, and an increasingly crowded – and confused – marketplace means that expert guidance is urgently needed. Enter two of Ireland's most respected young writers and bloggers, Caroline Hennessy and Kristin Jensen, and their fascinating and authoritative guide, a timely book that will be seized on by the growing army of discerning drinkers who are keen to find out which craft drinks they will most enjoy, especially when paired with their favourite foods. Even if you don't know a dunkel from an eisbock, anyone who enjoys real beer and cider should give this book a try – the fun is in the learning.' – GEORGINA CAMPBELL, food and hospitality writer, president of the Irish Food Writers' Guild and founder of the Georgina Campbell Guides

'The Irish craft beer revolution has been one of the most significant and successful movements in the history of Irish artisan food, and its dynamic story needed to be told authoritatively, and with humour and wit. Caroline Hennessy and Kristin Jensen are the perfect messengers for the revolution, able to report right from the heat of the mash tun before drawing back to view the history and development of brewing and cider-making throughout the country. It is the ambition of every author to wear your learning lightly, and in *Sláinte*, Caroline and Kristin deliver an encyclopedia's worth of information and knowledge, but do so in a book that has the lightness and grace of a missal.' – JOHN MCKENNA

For my Irish and NZ family, in particular my mother,
without whom there simply would not have been
enough hours in the day. – CH

For my husband Matt, who brought me to Ireland
for a one-year adventure – still here fifteen years later,
and what an adventure it has turned out to be with you. – KJ

SLÁINTE
First published 2014
by New Island
16 Priory Office Park
Stillorgan, Co. Dublin
www.newisland.ie

ISBN: 978-1-84840-374-1

British Library Cataloguing Data. A CIP catalogue record for this book is available from the British Library

Typeset by Mariel Deegan
Cover design and illustrations - www.thegreenmanstudio.com
Printed by Graficas Castuera, Spain

The authors wish to thank the following for their photographs:

Author photos: Joleen Cronin Photography (Caroline); Richard Hatch Photography (Kristin)

Beoir Chorca Dhuibhne page 91; Bord Bia pages 43, 124, 147, 153; Boyd Challenger page 98; Brú Brewery page 105; Burren Brewery page 93; Carlow Brewing Company pages 61, 87; Caroline Hennessy pages 8, 12, 13, 16, 36, 49, 75, 83, 116, 120, 141, 177, 181, 185, 187, 195; Clanconnel Brewing Company page 94; Dan Kelly's Cider pages 71, 77, 113; Declan Moore page 40; Donal Skehan pages 115, 136, 173; Dovehill Orchard pages 67, 113; Dungarvan Brewing Company page 96; Elbow Lane page 97; Imen McDonnell page 169; J.W. Sweetman pages 26, 58, 107, 132, 143; Karen Dempsey page 52; Kristin Jensen pages 114, 165; L. Mulligan Grocer page 139; Lily Ramirez-Foran page 191; Longueville House pages 84, 117; Mac Ivors pages 80, 117; Orpens Cider page 118; Seán O'Reilly | Toasty Oak pages 46, 204; Sheridans Cheesemongers page 154; Stonewell Cider page 119; The 5 Lamps Dublin Brewery page 102; The Apple Farm page 120; Toby's Handcrafted Cider page 121; White Gypsy page 103

10 9 8 7 6 5 4 3 2 1

Contents

sláinte (ˈslɑːntʃə) slaan-cheh. *noun*. From the Gaelic language, a drinking toast in Ireland that literally translates as 'health'. Synonyms: à votre santé, bottoms up, cheers, chin-chin, prost, salut, skål.

FOREWORD

There's been a virtual revolution in Ireland in the past couple of decades with the emergence of the artisan food sector. We've moved from being a nation of Calvita cheese eaters to a country with a growing pride in its produce and the skill of its cooks and chefs.

Food and travel writers wend their way down country lanes in search of local foods. They meet the makers – passionate, often deliciously eccentric characters – and are charmed. But what about the drinks? We have our famous beers, but those of us who have tasted the local brews in the UK and US wished we could find something similar closer to home, and the demand and craving grew. Tourists to Ireland also wondered why they couldn't find beers that were Irish, local and unique. The climate was right for yet another revolution. From 2007 onwards, microbreweries started to bubble up around the country, and the results were welcomed joyously.

Struggling pubs that had the vision to embrace the artisan and craft beers and ciders found their businesses booming. Craft breweries really took off, and the influential food writer John McKenna, author of *The Irish Food Guide*, predicted that matching food and Irish craft beers would be one of the hottest food trends in 2012 – how right he was. A growing number of top restaurants now have craft beer menus as well as a wine list and offer carefully chosen beer and food pairings. On a recent trip to Sweden, craft beer was served in wine glasses, topped up by the waiter and treated with the same reverence as a fine wine, and rightly so.

Many aspects of the craft beer and cider movement delight me: the passion and enthusiasm of the brewers, the extraordinary spirit of generosity and the sharing of ideas so rare in business nowadays. In just a few short years they have acquired a cult following of loyal fans and supporters who are obsessive about craft beer, who eagerly await the seasonal brews and, like sports fans, follow their favourite brewers and breweries to different festivals around the country.

The current bunch of microbrewers and cider-makers are a fascinating melange of IT workers, accountants, engineers, ex-bankers, plumbers and marine biologists who decided to follow their own dream and brew beer and make cider that they themselves would like to drink, and boy are they having fun.

The stories of the brewers and cider-makers, recounted so beautifully in this book, give us a glimpse into the life and fun times of the people behind the bottles. I love the chapter on cooking with beer and cider, the collection of tried and tested recipes, and of course the advice on food and beer/cider pairings and the particular focus on artisan producers and farmhouse cheese. The list of resources including beer festivals around the country and online shops where we can source our favourite brews is also invaluable. An intriguing book on a subject whose time has certainly come.

– Darina Allen, Ballymaloe Cookery School

INTRODUCTION

A revolution is happening in Ireland – a craft beer and cider revolution.

Go down to the pub, and you might spy a new tap on the bar. Rows of new bottles might have appeared on the shelf of your off-licence. When you're deciding what to drink at a restaurant, you might find a craft beer list in addition to the wine list. At a gastropub, the menu might even include suggestions for which beer or cider to match with each dish.

It wasn't always this way. Until a few years ago, every pub and every restaurant offered the same drinks from the same big brands. Yawn. But once the recession started to bite and pubs and restaurants started closing in droves, they quickly realised that they'd have to offer more choice and something different, and quickly, if they were to survive. Cue craft beer.

There are a lot of reasons why craft beer and cider are coming of age now in Ireland. The Irish food sector has been one of the few good news stories in the post-Celtic Tiger recession, continuing to grow despite the downturn, and craft beer is its poster child.

We are becoming more interested in and engaged with our food. Farmers' markets have cropped up all over the country and the calendar is jam-packed with food festivals, including several festivals dedicated solely to craft beer and cider. We have an insatiable appetite for TV cooking shows and cookbooks are still selling well even as other publishing categories decline. Instagram is awash with photos of perfectly poured cappuccinos and what people had for lunch. Food is the most pinned category on Pinterest and if you didn't tweet it, you didn't eat it. Everyone's a foodie now.

We also better understand the importance of supporting local and Irish businesses and we want to get better value for the money we spend, so we are willing to pay a little more for good-quality food and drink. Despite their products often being more expensive than their mass-produced counterparts, artisan food businesses report that, somewhat counter-intuitively, they're not only surviving, but thriving. There's no recession in good food and drink – we're all too busy eating our way through it.

In addition, with the advent of cheap flights (thanks, Ryanair!) and a two-holidays-a-year habit during the boom times, people's palates changed after travelling abroad, creating a new demand for pesto, Parma ham and imported olives. Ireland's gourmet food halls and delis are now stocked with sumac and za'atar, rosewater and rice paper wrappers, pomegranate molasses and fiery chillies. People who enjoyed real ale while travelling in the UK, proper cider while in France or hoppy microbrews in the US started wondering why they couldn't find something similar at home in Ireland. And on the flip side of the coin, tourists to Ireland increasingly ask what they can drink that's local and unique. After all, the famous big brands aren't even Irish owned any more.

We also have a growing international reputation for the quality of our food. Visiting food writers are in raptures over our cheese, dairy, butter, beef and bread – and, increasingly, our craft beer and cider.

While Brian Cowen's government might not have been good for much, one thing he did accomplish in 2005 was to lower the excise duty that microbreweries had to pay by 50%, which paved the way for the upsurge in brewery start-ups (most of Ireland's microbreweries have only come on stream since 2009) and allowed the few existing microbreweries to invest in new equipment and new beers.

To cap it all off, food writer John McKenna, author of *The Irish Food Guide*, predicted that matching food with Irish craft beers would be one of the hottest food trends in 2012, which had a positive effect on consumption according to Bord Bia, the Irish Food Board. 'Pubs are doomed unless they change their approach,' he said, adding, 'As the bigger breweries stumble, craft brewers thrive.'

This is a success story in the middle of a recession. Who would have thought that people would spend more money on a pint at a time when their income is dropping? But we are, and the microbrewing industry is growing at a rate of 45% a year in one of the worst recessions ever to hit Ireland. Gone are the days of mindlessly buying big brands; now consumers want to know that they're getting real bang for their buck, that what they spend their money on is really worth it. Why buy a slab of cans from an anonymous big brew when you can pick up a six pack from the brewery in your local town? You've met the brewers at several beer festivals, tweeted pictures of their beer, communicated with them on Facebook and they make something that you really enjoy drinking. These craft breweries are small, plucky Irish businesses that are making a go of it and succeeding against well-funded multinational beverage companies.

It's David and Goliath, but with mash tuns and apple presses instead of slingshots and stones.

The craft beer movement was quietly brewing in this climate since the mid 1990s; the cider side of things is a little more recent. But now it is finally stepping into the spotlight to slake our thirst and prove that Ireland has a lot more to offer than just the ubiquitous big brands.

Our beer backstory

For Kristin, it all started with the Dark Arts. When she moved to Ireland in 1999, she tried to like a certain famous stout. She was *determined* to like it. She kept ordering it in pubs in the hope that it might be an acquired taste, but she could only ever get halfway through the pint. She moved to Ireland in May but officially gave up on the black stuff by Christmas. It took her over ten years to realise that Guinness and stout are not one and the same. The light bulb moment came at a food festival beer tasting in 2011, when she was handed a cup of Trouble Brewing's Dark Arts porter. Instead of the metallic tang of Guinness, there was the taste of roasted coffee. A second sip revealed chocolate notes. Cue a *Green Eggs and Ham*-style revelation: Say! I *do* like stout! She's been making up for lost time ever since in exploring the magic that is beer and food matching. Come Friday night, you'll likely find her sitting at the kitchen table with her husband, sharing a beer and swapping notes on the taste and aroma – Is that grapefruit? Toffee? McVitie's biscuit? – and debating how well it matches with whatever is for dinner that night, be it chicken fajitas and an IPA, glazed ham and a cider, or a stout and a brownie for dessert.

Caroline used to live with Kiwi Scott and Aussie Cam in Dublin. For some reason she couldn't understand, they often complained about the sorry state of beer in Ireland. Seeing as this normally happened in a pub, it was easy to tell the boys to pipe down and drink their pints. Then she went to live in New Zealand. She could walk to two brewpubs from her house in Christchurch, choosing between a stroll down to the Dux de Lux for their legendary nachos and a glass of Nor'wester or heading over the river for pizza and a Golding Bitter at the

Twisted Hop. A Damascene conversion ensued. Scott wisely refrained from saying 'I told you so' and they spent much of their time in New Zealand researching local beers.

New Zealand was also the scene of another revelation. At a beer and food event, she tasted Speight's Porter with Whitestone Windsor Blue. The rich, nutty flavour of the beer, the intense, savoury cheese … taste buds exploded, a light went on and she quietly started to convince people that beer and food together made sense. But it had to be good beer, and initially that wasn't so easy to find when she returned to Ireland. Fortunately for her, that Kiwi and Aussie, now married to Irish girls (Caroline got Scott), stopped giving out about the beer on offer in Ireland and decided to make their own. In 2011 they launched Eight Degrees Brewing. Caroline hasn't been able to escape Irish craft beer or good cider ever since.

The Three Pillars of Enjoying Beer and Cider: Savour, Match, Cook

As we see it, there are three pillars to enjoying beer and cider: savouring it in its own right, matching it with food and using it in cooking.

A good craft beer or cider is something to savour, just like a good glass of wine. You don't need to become an expert, but you'd be surprised how even just a little knowledge about beer – from its ingredients (Chapter 1) or history (Chapter 2) to understanding its appearance, aroma, taste and texture – will increase your enjoyment of it. Serving it properly, in the right glass and at the right temperature (Chapter 3), takes it to the next level. Chapter 4, meanwhile, covers all the same aspects of cider.

If you drink craft beer and cider, you are already an active consumer. After all, you've had to go out and search for the stuff to begin with. You want to know more about what you're drinking, the people who make it and where you can find it. As with any artisan product, a lot of the appeal of craft beer and cider is not only the superior taste, but the people who make it and the stories behind it. These aren't anonymous, heartless beverages produced on a huge scale in some far-off factory, but locally made drinks that are the result of years of hard work from dedicated individuals. In Chapter 5, we profile the current brewers and cider-makers around Ireland to give you a taste of the personalities behind the bottles.

While a good beer or cider on its own is a fine thing, it will really shine when matched with the right food, so Chapter 6 offers some top tips on how to match what you're eating with what you're drinking to get the best of both worlds. Beer fully comes into its element as a social drink, which is why in Chapter 6 we have also listed some of the best pubs in which to enjoy a craft pint, the top gastropubs where you can enjoy a craft beer and a good meal together and the restaurants that take beer seriously. Wherever you are in the country, a good pint and some good grub probably aren't too far away. Meanwhile, Chapter 7 debunks the myth that wine and cheese are the perfect pairing. Believe it or not, beer is a much better match, and we offer our advice on matching Irish farmhouse cheese with Irish craft beer and cider. Your cheeseboard – and your palate – will never be the same again.

Chapter 8 outlines the principles of cooking with beer and cider and includes recipes from artisan food producers, restaurant owners, chefs, food writers and bloggers around Ireland, as well as some of our own tried and tested recipes.

The last section includes a list of resources for everything from beer festivals around the country to online retailers that stock a good range of Irish craft beers and ciders and that deliver nationwide. Want to know your ABV from your IBU? The glossary outlines some of the most common terms you will encounter when talking about beer and cider.

It is an exciting and dynamic time for discerning drinkers in Ireland, with a world of craft beer and cider waiting to be discovered, one savoured sip at a time. *Sláinte*!

Part one

SAVOUR

CHAPTER 1

WHAT IS BEER?

Beer is an alcoholic beverage made from four essential ingredients: malted barley, hops, yeast and lots and lots of water – but it's what the brewer does with these ingredients that counts. Brewers are like chefs and need to choose their ingredients carefully: crystal malt or chocolate malt? Cascade hops or Ella hops? What kind of beer does he or she want to make? Will it be an ultra-hoppy, thirst-quenching IPA (India pale ale) or something deeply dark and satisfyingly traditional, like a stout?

It starts off simple but gets very complicated, very fast. Each of the key ingredients has a role to play in how the beer will turn out. And then there are the add-ons, called adjuncts: rye, oats, even coffee and spices like vanilla, coriander and cumin can all be included at different stages in the brew to make something lip-smackingly delicious. The brewer constantly has to keep in mind the overall balance of the flavour of the beer. To push the hop levels, there has to be a malt to underpin the flavours. On the other hand, a dark, malty beer still needs some hops to spike the flavours and keep it from being too cloying.

Ingredients

Malt
Malted barley – or malt – is the main body of the beer. It provides the sugars for fermentation and gives colour to the beer along with sweet, biscuity flavours and aromas to balance the hops.

Barley is the fourth most commonly grown cereal in the world (after wheat, maize and rice) and is widely grown in Ireland. Dick Walsh of Cork's Malting Company of Ireland has noticed a real demand for Irish malt, beginning ten years ago when they started to supply the Franciscan Well. The company now supplies malt to around ten of the bigger Irish micro-breweries. As a result of increased interest from microbreweries and home brewers for small volumes of malt, they now sell it in 25kg bags.

> *'Malt does more than Milton can to justify God's ways to man.'*
> *– A.E. Housman*

While barley also goes to the animal feed industry, the best barley is used for malting, which turns its starch into accessible sugars for brewing. It's a start–stop process. First, the maltster – the person who makes malt – steeps the barley in water and allows it to start germinating. Then it is dried, which stops the germination process and produces kernels of malted barley.

Different styles of malt are produced by varying the temperature and length of time at each stage of the process. This lets brewers choose from a maltster's palette of colours and flavours, from the light gold of pale malt to dark roasted chocolate malt.

Depending on the style of the beer they are brewing and the colour and the flavour that they hope to achieve, brewers must choose their malt carefully. Irish malt is used alongside a selection of speciality malt from countries like England, Germany and the US. Each variety of malt does a different job, affecting the colour, flavour, aroma and even the mouthfeel of the beer.

Base malt

Base malts make up the majority of the ingredients used in a particular brew. Different varieties of barley are used. One of the best known is Maris Otter, an English barley that was bred to produce high-quality malt for the British cask ale industry in the 1960s. Propino is one of the types of barley grown for malting in Ireland. Lighter-coloured malts, like pale malt and pilsner malt, are also used as base malts, as they provide a high level of fermentable sugars for the yeast to transform into alcohol.

Speciality malt

This is where it starts to get really interesting. These malts are used, in smaller amounts than the base malts, to produce the specific flavours and aromas of coffee, chocolate and caramel and to give colour and body to the brew. Ask any brewery to tell you which malt they are using and they will reel off a litany of names of the different malts that they have mixed to make exactly the kind of beer they want.

Uses and flavours of malt

Base malt	
Pale malt	An important base malt for ale, with delicate flavours of biscuit and toast and a light colour.
Pilsner malt	Used as a base malt, particularly for pilsners and lagers. Contributes a golden colour.
Speciality malt	
Crystal or caramel malt	A range of malts available in different colours, with rich flavours that vary from sweet toffee to deep caramel. They contribute body, sweetness and a reddish colour to beer.
Roasted malt	The variety of colours comes from the kilning or roasting process, from the toasty Munich malt (a base malt for bock-style beer) to chocolate malt (dark chocolate flavour, used in porters and stouts) and smoky black malt.

Other grains	
Roasted barley	Unmalted, but heated until it is almost black. It gives a burnt coffee or chocolate flavour to dark beers, and it is particularly important for the dry flavour of a traditional Irish stout and in helping the beer to retain its trademark foamy head.
Raw barley	Unmalted, often flaked. Gives stouts a distinctive richness.
Wheat	Good for head retention and body. Used for witbier and hefeweizen.
Oats	Occasionally used in stout for a creamy, smooth mouthfeel.
Rye	Traditionally used in roggenbier, and now sometimes used in brewing pale ales (Rye-P-As!) for a characteristic dry, spicy flavour.
Corn, rice	A source of cheap fermentable sugars frequently used in commercial American beers. Gives a lighter flavour than malt.
Sorghum	A gluten-free grain used to brew GF beer.

'Adjunct: Any carbohydrate source other than malt that contributes fermentable sugars to the wort (usually less expensive than barley malt).'
– The Institute of Brewing and Distilling, London

While only malt, hops, yeast and water are necessary to make beer, that doesn't always mean the brewer stops there. Adjuncts can be a dirty word: mass-market beers are frequently brewed using corn or rice to reduce the cost of brewing. In craft brewing, however, adjuncts are added to enhance the end product or to brew a particular style of beer.

Dungarvan Brewing produces a seasonal rye IPA (Rye-P-A) called Mahon Falls Rye Pale Ale. Kinnegar Brewing's Rustbucket is another rye ale, combining spice notes with citrusy hops. Wheat is also used to brew – guess what? – wheat beers, like Carlow Brewing's tart and fruity Curim Gold. Things like spices, chocolate, fruit or vegetables are all popular additions to seasonal brews like pumpkin beers or winter ales.

Hops

Think of hops as the spice in brewing. While only a small amount of hops are used in the recipe (normally between 70g and 700g per 100 litres), they are essential for their bitterness, flavour, aroma and preservative qualities.

Hops are the flowers of a perennial plant called *Humulus lupulus* and look like soft green pine cones. Hop flowers aren't exactly what you'd pick for a bouquet, being pale green and tending to fade discretely into the background, but these humble blossoms pack a huge punch. Rich in essential oils, alpha acids and resins, they impart a variety of flavour and aroma profiles, like citrus, spice, grass, pine, flowers and wood.

While they are native to central Europe, a few hop varieties, such as Fuggle and Northern Brewer, were produced commercially in Ireland during the 1960s by four growers, including Edgar Calder-Potts of Highbank Orchards (father of Rod Calder-Potts, who now makes cider; see page 114). The government at the time introduced a measure obliging Guinness to buy these Irish hops before importing hops from Guinness's own farms in Kent, Sussex and Worcestershire. After Ireland joined the EEC in 1973, however, the government was no longer able to maintain preferential treatment for Irish hops and the market gradually petered out. But now, with an interest in producing all-Irish beer made from locally grown ingredients, brewers like White Gypsy's Cuilán Loughnane and Gordon Fallis of Inishmacsaint Brewing are growing their own.

The potential of hops is what really gets brewers excited, and they like to shout about it. Take a look at your nearest bottle of craft beer – many will list the hops that have been used, and some of the beers are even named after the hop, such as Porterhouse's Hersbrucker Pilsner or the Green Bullet Pale Ale from Mountain Man. Each hop variety has a distinctive

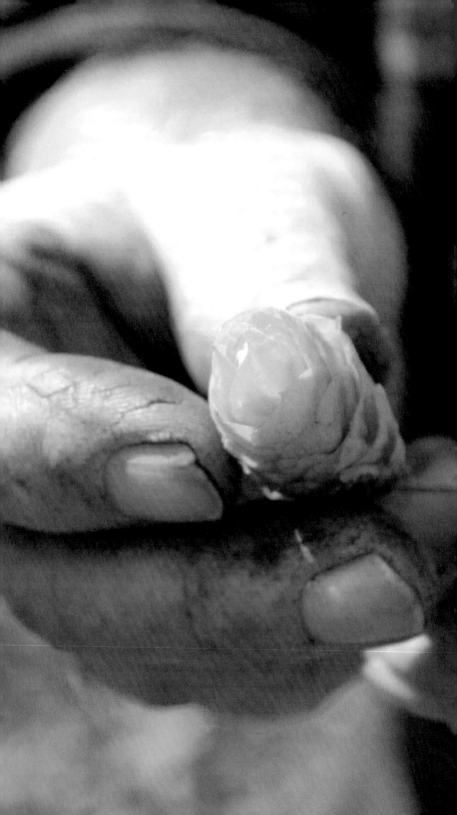

flavour profile – think about wine grape varietals and how different Merlot is to Pinot Noir – and with a little bit of knowledge you'll soon find yourself distinguishing between the flowery American Cascade and the peppery Saaz, a Czech native.

Different hops drift in and out of fashion, as cutting-edge craft breweries are constantly on the lookout for new and exciting varieties. Traditional English hops with fantastically Hobbit-like names such as Fuggle and Golding, Phoenix and Boadicea, while still being used, are often left in the shade by New World hops from America, Australia and New Zealand.

New Zealand hops

Growing hops are a glorious sight. Anyone who has ever driven the road between Motueka and Riwaka in New Zealand's South Island will have seen fields of hop bines (known as hop gardens) that have been trained to grow up to four metres high on wires strung between tall poles. With the grapey Sauvignon Blanc-like flavour of Nelson Sauvin as the flagship, NZ hops are creating quite a stir on this side of the world, with breweries eager to shout about these new hops in their beers.

New Zealand Hops is a seventeen-strong growers' co-operative based in Nelson in the heart of the Tasman Bay hop-growing area, and they're producing first-class aroma hops like the lemon–lime Motueka, the grapefruit citrus of Riwaka and the passionfruit of Rakau. Put those together with intriguing bittering hops, such as Pacific Gem's blackberry and pine notes, or the lemon peel and pine needle of Southern Cross, and you have the tools to create good, flavoursome, interesting beers.

Hop alphabet, from Amarillo to Zeus

Variety	Characteristics
Amarillo	Sweet spices and oranges – good for dry hopping
Cascade	Bold grapefruit notes that have become associated with American IPAs
Centennial	Lots of citrus aroma and flavour, similar to Cascade
Citra	Strong flavours of citrus and tropical fruit
Columbus	Citrus and resin – can be used for bittering as well as aroma
Dr Rudi	From New Zealand – gives a crisp, bitter flavour with a little resin character
Ella	Australian hop with floral and fruity characteristics
First Gold	English dwarf hop with floral and tangerine notes – grown by White Gypsy in Co. Tipperary
Fuggle	Traditional English hop, earthy and vegetal
Golding	English hop with delicate spicy and floral notes
Green Bullet	NZ bittering hop that's equally at home in a lager or a traditional dry stout

Using hops

If you cook with spices, you know that the final flavour depends on the point at which you add them to the dish. It is exactly the same with hops. There are three different stages for adding hops when making beer. Early in the brewing process, bittering hops like Willamette and Golding are added because the boiling enables the conversion of their alpha acids, contributing a crisp bite to the beer. Aroma and flavouring hops (think

Variety	Characteristics
Hallertauer	One of Germany's noble hops, which are European varieties with high aroma and low bitterness – this one has mild grass and spice notes
Mosaic	Tangerine, tropical fruit and blueberry flavours
Motueka	Strong lemon and lime citrus aroma and tropical fruit flavours
Nelson Sauvin	From New Zealand – imparts juicy, fruity, Sauvignon Blanc-like flavours
Riwaka	Citrus and passionfruit
Saaz	A noble hop from the Czech Republic with a peppery, spicy bite – used in pilsner
Simcoe	American hop with pine and passionfruit flavours
Sorachi Ace	Japanese hop with distinctive aromas of lemon zest and coconut
Willamette	An American take on Fuggle, with blackcurrant and herbal aromas
Zeus	Aromatic American hop with citrus and resin notes

Simcoe and Cascade), on the other hand, are added in towards the end of the boil to impart their flavour profiles to the beer.

The third – optional – stage is called dry hopping. This involves adding hops to the beer at a low temperature after fermentation, when they are left to infuse the beer for a few days or even up to several weeks. This technique boosts hop aroma and flavour without the bitterness that is drawn out by heat.

IBUs

Sometimes it seems like craft beer is full of acronyms, and god help you if you mix up your IBUs and your IPAs. IBUs are international bitterness units. They measure the perceived bitterness in beer (so IBUs are in the IPAs) and give you an approximate idea of how hoppy the beer is. Each IBU is one milligram of isomerised alpha acids per litre of beer. For instance, American IPAs vary between forty and seventy IBUs, while a Russian imperial stout weighs in between fifty and ninety. But because the Russian imperial stout has more malt and alcohol per litre as well, the bitterness is not as evident on your palate. In general, though, a beer with a low IBU will taste less bitter than a beer with a high IBU.

Playing with hops

A hop randall is a filter that is filled with hops and attached to a draught line, which enables brewers or bar staff to boost the hops while the beer is pouring. The real fun is in using different hops with the same beer. Blacks of Kinsale brought a randall to the 2013 Irish Craft Beer and Cider Festival and the Vanguard Beer Collective now has a randall that they are rotating in pubs around the country – follow it on  Twitter (@VanguardRandall) to see where it's currently pouring. Think of it as a cafetière for hops – although according to Sam Black, you don't want to be the one who has to clean it out!

Yeast

Yeast is yeast is yeast, right? Wrong!

Without yeast, beer would be missing an essential element: alcohol. The brewer needs the yeast to get the fermentation process moving, turning all those super-sweet malt sugars into something drinkable. Human control over this is relatively recent. It wasn't until the mid 1800s that French microbiologist Louis Pasteur proved that yeast is a single-celled micro-organism that reproduces by budding. Before that, yeast was known to brewers as 'god-is-good', which seems like a prayer to whoever is out there that fermentation would actually work on brew day.

With knowledge comes power. Brewers were able to select the best strains to create their own yeast cultures and make the beer that they wanted to make instead of the kind that resulted from spontaneous fermentation – and boy did they make it work.

Top-fermenting: These ale yeasts ferment rapidly (ale fermentation may only take a few days) at warm temperatures (between 10°C and 25°C), producing complex fruity and spicy flavours and aromas. The yeast rises to the top of the fermentation vessel, creating a rich, thick yeast head, which in past times would have been skimmed off and pitched into the next brew. Ale, porter, stout, wheat beer and kölsch are made with top-fermenting yeast.

Bottom-fermenting: These strains of yeast work best at cooler temperatures (7°C to 15°C). This means that the yeast takes more time to ferment – up to twice as long as ale yeast – before it settles at the bottom of the fermenter. The beer still needs to be finished by storing it (*lagerung* in German, from which the word 'lager' is derived) at a low temperature and allowing it to age for weeks or months to let the yeast finish off the job, producing a clean, crisp beer. Lager, pilsner, märzen, dortmunder and bock use bottom-fermenting yeast.

Other yeasts: Although brewers can and do want to control fermentation, the age-old process of spontaneous fermentation is still used for particular styles of beer. This involves allowing wild yeasts to ferment the beer, in a similar way to making a sourdough starter from just flour and water. The slow-growing *Brettanomyces lambicus*, colloquially known as Brett, is the name of a wild yeast used in this style of brewing, especially for funky Belgian-style sour, unfiltered lambic beers or gueuze. It is also possible to buy tamed – and more predictable – versions of these from a yeast lab. Wild fermentation takes time and can be unpredictable, but offers an intense and complex range of flavours.

In 2013, the state of Oregon in the US designated the brewer's yeast *Saccharomyces cerevisiae* the official state microbe in recognition of its key role in the state's economy. Portland has more breweries than any other city in the world and the state's craft beer industry is currently worth $2.4 billion. Dublin has some catching up to do.

Water

Not all water tastes the same. Beer is mainly water, so brewers pay considerable attention to where it comes from. In the past, the quality of the water available to breweries was what gave birth to the different beer styles. The hard, sulphate-infused water at Burton-on-Trent in England was responsible for the sharpness of the original India pale ale, while Dublin's hard water is ideal for brewing porter. Dundalk, with its low-alkaline water, was the home of Harp lager. Brewers tended to concentrate on one specific style, dictated by the water that they had access to.

Although there are a few breweries, like Beoir Chorca Dhuibhne, who have their own well, most breweries' water supply comes ready-treated from their local council. Brewers can then adjust the mineral content as needed so that they are not limited to one style of beer.

'Not all chemicals are bad. Without chemicals such as hydrogen and oxygen, for example, there would be no way to make water, a vital ingredient in beer.'

– Dave Barry, American journalist and author

The Brewing Process

Once the brewer has decided on what style of beer they want to make, they need to finalise their recipe and measure out the ingredients – just like any cook in the kitchen. Sacks of malt are ready to go, hops have been chosen and the yeast is raring for action. Now it's time to get stuck into some real work, because brewing is a hard, physical activity with lots of brewing-specific terms and plenty of stainless steel to play with.

There are four stages of brewing: mashing, brewing, fermenting and conditioning.

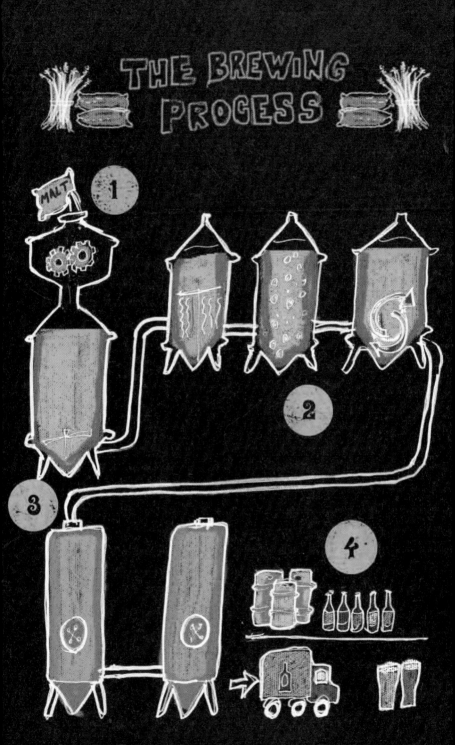

brew kettle: The container in which wort is boiled together with the hops and any other flavourings or adjuncts that are being added at that stage.

conditioning: Ageing and maturing are synonymous terms for conditioning, which refers to the time needed for a beer to become the best version of itself. Conditioning includes bottle conditioning, cask conditioning and lagering.

gravity: The density of the wort, which is measured at two distinct stages. Original gravity is the density of the wort compared to water before the beer starts fermenting. It measures how much sugar is in the wort, which is a good indicator of how alcoholic the final beer will be. Final gravity is the density measurement after the beer has finished fermenting. The alcoholic strength of the beer can be calculated by the difference between the original gravity and the final gravity.

lauter tun: The vessel in which the sweet wort is separated from the mash by allowing the liquid to drain away through thin slits in the bottom that act as a sieve. The mash is then sparged in the lauter tun to extract most of the sugar from the grain.

lautering: The process of separating the mash from the sweet wort in the mash tun or lauter tun. There are three steps in lautering: mashout, recirculation and sparging.

racking: Drawing the beer off the spent yeast sediment and transferring it to another vessel.

secondary fermentation: A type of ageing or conditioning that takes place in a fresh container after racking the beer. It can take anywhere from several weeks to months. Bottle-conditioned beer and cask ales undergo a secondary fermentation.

sparging: The step in lautering where hot water is gently sprinkled through the grain to extract every last bit of sugar. To help you visualise it, some home brewers use a watering can for this step.

wort: When the malted barley (or other grain) is steeped in hot water in the mash tun, the resulting sugar-rich amber liquid is wort.

1. Mashing

Malted barley – sometimes milled at the brewery, sometimes sourced pre-milled – is mixed with hot water into a kind of a porridge, or mash, which allows the enzymes in the malt to break down the starches and proteins. This process takes place in a vessel called the mash tun, with the brewer controlling the time and temperature. While all that's going on, the brewery smells like … well, like a sweet, warm, fuggy brewery.

When the malt starches have been converted into sugar, this sweet solution, now called wort, needs to be separated from the malt barley husks. This is called the lautering (or separation) stage, and it can take place in the mash tun or in another stainless steel vessel called a lauter tun. The first sweet, syrupy wort is pumped back over top of the malt to clarify the wort. Once the wort is running clear it is steadily pumped over to the kettle, while at the same time the grains are sprayed with hot water to sparge, or rinse out, any leftover sugars.

The wort is pumped into the brew kettle while someone at the brewery – often the smallest person or someone on work experience – is sent into the mash or lauter tun to shovel out the steaming spent grain. In home brewing, this can be used for making bread or muffins, but with anything from 150kg to 500kg of it being produced in a microbrewery per brew, it often goes to a local farmer for the cattle or pigs to fight over. At farm-based breweries, like Mescan Brewery and West Mayo Brewery, the spent grain can be fed straight to their own animals.

> Sarah Roarty from the N17 Brewery believes in getting as much value from the brewing process as possible, and that includes the spent grains. You can find her recipe for spent grain granola bars on page 182.

2. Brewing

The wort is brought to a rolling boil in the brew kettle and the first (bittering) hops are added. Boiling the wort sterilises it, along with converting and dissolving the bitter alpha acids from the hops. This stage takes between one and two hours, the brewer carefully observing and judging the right time to add the aroma hops. That done, the brewer then creates a whirlpool to settle the hop matter and pumps the wort through a heat exchanger into the fermentation tanks.

3. Fermenting

As soon as yeast is added to the cooled, bittersweet wort, fermentation begins. All the hard work in converting malt starches into fermentable sugars finally pays off as the yeast converts them into alcohol and carbon dioxide. The timeframe for this stage depends on whether the brewer is making ale or lager. Ale fermentation happens quickly. This creates heat, but the tanks have cooling jackets that maintain the temperature between 19°C and 24°C and also prevent the development of esters (unwanted fruity flavours). With lager, fermentation is a slower process and the temperature is kept between 10°C and 15°C throughout.

4. Conditioning

When the beer is at the right gravity, it's time to cool it down and remove the yeast. After all that hard work, the beer needs to rest. But it's not all beauty sleep. This is when dry hopping can take place (a final addition of aroma hops left to steep in the beer).

Ale gets conditioned for just a couple of weeks in the tank. It can then be filtered to remove some of the yeast, leaving the beer clear without removing too much flavour. It can also be carbonated by adding carbon dioxide gas before being kegged or bottled. Alternatively, it can be cask or bottle conditioned, meaning the beer goes straight in from the fermenter to complete the conditioning process, sometimes with a little extra yeast or sugar to enhance the natural carbonation.

Lager needs to be conditioned for three to four weeks. It has already had a slow, cold fermentation, and now it undergoes a slow, cold conditioning, which develops its characteristic crisp freshness.

Go nitro

You can drink mainstream stouts like Guinness for years and not know where that rich, creamy head and smooth mouthfeel come from. That's nitrogenation, or nitro, which refers to the nitrogen gas used in the carbonation process. It's not widely used by microbreweries, the exception being Brú Dubh Nitro Stout, so don't expect the same lingering head in a craft beer as you'll find on mainstream stouts.

Beer Styles in Ireland

Knowing the style of a beer will help you to make an informed choice about what you're drinking. Style refers to the way the beer is made, the balance between malt and hops, and the alcohol strength (alcohol by volume, or ABV) and gives you an idea of what flavours to expect in your glass. All beer falls into one of just two families: top-fermented ales or bottom-fermented lagers. (For more on the differences between the two, turn to page 17.)

While in theory there is a vast array of styles available to Irish micro-breweries, in practice most of them stick with a holy trinity of three core beers: a pale ale, a red ale and a porter or stout. Other popular styles are lagers, stout variations and wheat beers. These signature brews are the solid backbone of the brewery, the reliable beers that pay the bills. The limited edition seasonal special is when brewers get to play with new styles and hops and create something that might be around for only one release.

Ale or beer?

Ale is beer, lager is beer, porter is beer – it's all beer. (Except if you're drinking wine – you've got the wrong book.) 'While "ale" was the most common name for our beloved beverage, "beer" was also used by the Anglo-Saxons from about the sixth or seventh century,' says Pete Brown in *Man Walks into a Pub*. 'This word derives from the Latin *biber*, "a drink", which in turn comes from *bibere*, "to drink". Beer was so vital, its very name was synonymous with drink in its broadest sense.'

Lager and pilsner

While big-brand lagers – pale yellow, sweet, vaguely hoppy – dominated the Irish market for many years, the micros now produce a solid selection of balanced, quaffable alternatives. True lagers or pilsners are dry and crisp, with a distinctive hop bitterness and a character that comes from the use of malted barley rather than corn or rice. Porterhouse Hersbrucker Pilsner has a malty sweetness with floral notes from the German noble hop Hersbrucker, a hop that they also include in their 'genuine Irish lager', Temple Bräu. Dublin Lager from The 5 Lamps has a nice peppery spice flavour from another noble hop, Saaz.

Pale ale

Pale ale was originally an English style, golden to deep copper in colour, with moderate hop bitterness from traditional English hops. The term 'bitter' was used for an unfiltered cask-conditioned pale ale. The category has now broadened, and there's India pale ale, American pale ale, Belgian pale ale and, some might say, Irish pale ale.

Most microbreweries in Ireland make their own pale ale. Predominantly pale ale malts are used, often with American hops. It is a diverse style, with moderate to high hop bitterness, citrus and floral notes, and a refreshingly drinkable bitterness to the finish. Galway Hooker Brewery, Carlow Brewing and Clanconnel all brew what they have named Irish pale ale.

India pale ale (IPA)

Want to export beer to the denizens of the British Empire in India in an era before refrigeration? Brew with lots of hops and at a high alcohol level to ensure that it survives a six-month ocean voyage, plenty of temperature fluctuations and lots of sloshing around in a ship's hold. While considerable amounts of other beer styles were sent to India – porter was also popular, according to *The Oxford Companion to Beer* – IPA has become known as the beer of the British Empire.

Red ale

Although there is some dissent, red ale has become known as a traditional Irish style. It varies from amber in colour to a deep red or copper. It has some sweet caramel malt flavours with toffee or toasted notes and tends to be lightly hopped. This is a style that particularly showcases cara and crystal malts, from light caramel through to dark toffee. Some breweries use a touch of roasted barley to give a burnt malt counterbalance to the sweetness. One of the more traditional examples is White Gypsy's Ruby Red, while Copper Coast from Dungarvan Brewing has a more pronounced fruitiness that works beautifully with the toffee flavour. Craft breweries have recently evolved this style further, adding a noticeable hop bitterness to counterbalance the sweetness. For example, Eight Degrees Brewing uses Pacifica hops for a citrus and floral aroma in its Sunburnt Irish Red.

Porter and stout

Porter or stout? This is one of those questions that crops up regularly at beer events or over a few pints of something dark. They are both beers made with a balance towards dark malt rather than hops, using top-fermenting ale yeasts.

But which came first? Porter has the edge there. An English style that originated in the eighteenth century, London porter was a strong, dark beer that got its name from its popularity amongst street market porters and other labourers. By the end of the 1700s, there was an active and profitable export trade of London porter from England to Ireland, peaking at an annual export of 125,000 barrels (4.5 million gallons) in 1793. Irish breweries took up the challenge, and Beamish & Crawford's Cork Porter Brewery was established in 1792. By 1805 it was the largest brewery in Ireland, producing 100,000 barrels per annum, and it was the third-largest brewery in the then United Kingdom.

Because it was such a popular style, breweries used to produce different strengths of porter. The term 'stout' – as in extra stout porter or stout porter – was used to denote a beer that was stronger. At some stage during the 1800s the prefix was dropped and stout became increasingly dominant in the market. There are now many styles of stout: chocolate, coffee, dry (or Irish), foreign extra, imperial, milk, oatmeal and oyster.

Porter was gradually abandoned by breweries, with last-brewery-standing Guinness dropping it from their roster in 1973, before microbreweries like Hilden and Porterhouse revived the style in Ireland in the late twentieth century. Porter often has a lighter body than stout, with low to moderate hop flavour and a roasted, malty character. Trouble Brewing's Dark Arts Porter comes in at 4.4% ABV, with complex notes of coffee and dark chocolate.

Nowadays, thanks to Guinness's marketing department, stout is the style of beer most associated with Ireland. Irish dry stout is a full-flavoured brew, almost black in the glass, with plenty of roasted flavours, a creamy mouthfeel and a very dry finish. But it is no longer the stronger of the two in terms of ABV. Hilden Irish Stout is a good example of this traditional style, as is Black Rock Stout from Dungarvan Brewing, both coming in at 4.3% ABV.

Special stout

If there's a beer style, there's a brewer who wants to push it to the next degree, producing what we call special stouts. Porterhouse make a rich, dark, imperial Celebration Stout (7% ABV), while their popular Oyster Stout has a slight mineral tang from the fresh oysters added to the brew kettle at the end of the boil. Carlow Brewing's Leann Folláin, at 6%, is a full-flavoured, complex, chocolate-and-molasses stout. In addition, Carlow Brewing, the Franciscan Well and Eight Degrees all released limited edition high-alcohol barrel-aged stouts in 2013.

Wheat beer

These pale, refreshing beers are brewed with a substantial amount of wheat, are generally top-fermented and can often be unfiltered. For German-style weissbier (white beer) or weizenbier (wheat beer), a special yeast is used to give trademark flavours of bananas, cloves and even

bubblegum. Try Friar Weisse from the Franciscan Well for a real banana hit; O'Hara's Curim Gold has notes of plum and peach; and White Gypsy's Blond has green apple and clove-like aromas. Belgium brings the witbier style to the table, using coriander and orange peel for extra fruit and spice flavours. Drink these beers while young and properly chilled on a hot summer's day for best effect.

Style	Characteristics	Three to Try
Lager and pilsner	Pale gold colour, dry and crisp, with a distinctive hop bitterness	5 Lamps Dublin Lager Porterhouse Temple Bräu Whitewater Brewery Belfast Lager
Pale ale	Golden colour, moderate to high hop bitterness, with citrus and floral notes	Galway Hooker J. W. Sweetman Pale Ale McGraths Irish Pale Ale #2
Red ale	Amber to deep red, sweet caramel malt flavours, with toffee or toasted notes	Brú Rua Hilden Halt White Gypsy Ruby Red
Porter	Porter is lighter in body than stout, with low to moderate hop flavour and a roasted, malty character	Galway Bay Brewery Stormy Port J. W. Sweetman Porter Trouble Brewing Dark Arts Porter
Stout	A full-flavoured brew, almost black in the glass, with plenty of roasted flavours, a creamy mouthfeel and a dry finish	Dungarvan Brewing Black Rock Stout Franciscan Well Shandon Stout McGrath's Irish Black Stout #4
Special stouts	Pushing the traditional stout barriers	O'Hara's Leann Folláin Porterhouse Oyster Stout Porterhouse Wrasslers 4X
Wheat beer	Pale and refreshing, sometimes cloudy, with banana, clove and bubblegum flavours	Franciscan Well Friar Weisse O'Hara's Curim Gold White Gypsy Blond

An A to Z of Beer Styles

Lager accounts for 90% of all beer consumed, but there are more than eighty different beer styles brewed around the world. Here's a taste of just a few of them. You'll often find that Irish breweries have their own interpretations of these.

altbier: A copper-coloured, slightly fruity ale with some of the clean, crisp characteristics of a lager, altbier means 'old beer' in German and is the hallmark style of Düsseldorf.

barley wine: A type of strong ale (8–15% ABV) that was originally brewed in England. American brewers also make barley wines now, though they tend to be hoppier and hence more bitter than British barley wines, which are on the sweeter side.

blonde ale: A light ale ranging in colour from straw to deep golden that is only slightly bitter and a bit toasty in flavour. A good introduction for someone just starting to explore the world of craft beers.

bitter: The quintessential British beer, bitter is a pale ale that is subdivided into three categories based on ABV: standard or ordinary bitter (up to 4.1%), best or regular bitter (4.2–4.7%) and premium or strong bitter, also known as extra special bitter (ESB) (4.8% and up). Contrary to what the name might suggest, bitters are actually very drinkable, well-balanced beers.

bock: A smooth, strong, dark, malty and slightly sweet German lager. *Ein bock* means 'a billy goat' in German and is a play on the town name of Einbeck, where bock was first brewed, which is why you'll sometimes see a goat logo used on these beers.

brown ale: A mild ale that ranges in colour from copper to deep brown or mahogany and has a sweet, nutty, malty flavour with hints of toffee.

cream ale: An ale version of American lager, designed to be light, crisp and refreshing, with no pronounced hop or malt flavours one way or another.

doppelbock: A double bock, which, as the name suggests, is stronger and more alcoholic than a regular bock (7–12% ABV). It is rich and sweet, with pronounced malty, toasty flavours. First brewed by Paulaner friars in the 1700s in Munich, it was their 'liquid bread' during periods of fasting.

dubbel: A fruity, slightly bitter dark brown Trappist ale that is quite strong at 6–8% ABV.

dunkel: A catch-all term that describes several different types of dark, malty Bavarian and German lagers. The word *dunkel* means 'dark' in German, which is why you'll also sometimes see it used as a prefix for another style, such as dunkelweizen (a dark wheat beer).

eisbock: These dark lagers are frozen towards the end of their maturation period, creating a very smooth, very malty and very strong beer (around 10% ABV).

faro: A type of lambic sweetened with brown sugar, caramel or molasses to take the sour edge off. A good aperitif beer.

framboise/frambozenbier: A type of lambic made with raspberries.

geuze/gueuze: A dry, sour Belgian beer made by blending young and old lambics and then bottling it for a secondary fermentation. Unlike a straight-up lambic, which is flat, a geuze has some sparkle.

helles: A straw-coloured, sparklingly clear (in German, *helles* means 'bright') Munich lager with a tall, creamy head, a mildly malty taste, just a little spicy hop bite and a dry finish.

imperial: The word 'imperial' is used to denote bigger, bolder, fuller-flavoured versions of the original style (such as imperial stout) with a higher ABV. Imperial beers are all about *more*: more malt, more hops, more flavour, more alcohol.

IPA: India pale ale, a style of highly hopped strong ale that came about in the late 1700s, when beer brewed in England was shipped to India by sea.

kölsch: A smooth, crisp, light ale noted for its sparkling clarity and delicate, slightly fruity, well-balanced flavour.

kriek: A type of lambic that has sour cherries added to it.

lambic: A dry, flat, sour, wheat-based Belgian ale that is spontaneously fermented with wild yeast. There are three types of lambic: fruit (such as kriek or framboise), geuze and faro.

mild ale: A type of English brown ale with an emphasis on the malt. One to try if you're not a fan of bitter beer.

Oktoberfest: Also known as märzen, an amber lager that is malty, toasty and smooth, yet also retains the clean characteristics of a lager, with a dark gold to deep orange-red colour.

pumpkin ale: An autumn seasonal that incorporates pumpkins in the brew and spices like cinnamon, cloves, nutmeg, allspice and ground ginger.

quadrupel: The strongest of the Trappist ales, with an ABV of around 10% or more. It has a sweet, fruity, almost sherry-like flavour, a dark colour and a heavy body – this is a serious, super-strong beer.

rye beer: Any beer where some rye has been used in place of barley, resulting in a slight spiciness in the beer.

saison: A refreshing, hoppy, pale Belgian farmhouse ale with some fruity and spicy notes too. It was originally brewed in the winter and then set aside to be enjoyed in the hot summer months.

Scotch ale: Strong Scotch ale is also known as wee heavy, with an ABV to match the moniker (usually 6.5–10%). These copper-coloured ales have a rich, malty, caramel sweetness.

Trappist ale: Trappist ale has a protected designation of origin – for starters, it must actually be brewed within the walls of a Trappist monastery. There are three styles of Trappist ale: dubbel, tripel and quadrupel.

tripel: A fruity, spicy, strong, golden Trappist ale with an ABV of around 9%.

Vienna lager: A reddish-brown, toasty, malty, slightly sweet lager. The style may have died out in its native Vienna, but it is still made in Mexico, where it was brought by Austrian immigrant brewers in the late 1800s.

wheat wine: A variation of barley wine that was developed in the US in the 1980s.

wild ale: The Marmite of beer – you either love it or hate it. It is brewed with wild yeasts or bacteria, giving it a sour, funky vibe.

zoigl: A beer that is only brewed in the Upper Palatinate region of eastern Bavaria, traditionally brewed communally.

Beer Is Good for You!

In bottle-conditioned beers like those from Dungarvan Brewing and Beoir Chorca Dhuibhne, you'll come across a yeast sediment in the dregs of the bottle. Don't just tip that down the drain: it contains B vitamins, amino acids and minerals – a nicer way of getting your recommended daily allowance than taking a pill.

Wine may have been doing a good PR job for quite some time, but studies at Italy's Fondazione di Ricerca e Cura have shown that moderate consumption of beer or wine – the key word here being *moderate* – is associated with reduced risk of cardiovascular disease. The amount that the Italian researchers recommend is about a pint a day. If you're drinking craft beer, you're getting the full-flavour bang for your pint buck.

Add to that the fact that beer has as many antioxidants as wine (albeit different ones, from barley and hops rather than grapes), along with dietary silicon, more protein and B vitamins, and it looks like beer drinkers are onto a winner.

> *'In both England and Ireland, stout was widely considered a healthful tonic ... the Irish even referred to stout as "mother's milk" and prescribed it to nursing mothers, who were supposed to benefit from its high iron content (and, no doubt, babies benefited from tastier milk).'*
> – Garrett Oliver, The Brewmaster's Table *(2003)*

What Is Craft Beer?

Craft, like *artisan*, *farmhouse* and *home-made*, is not a legal term. *Microbrewery*, on the other hand, does have a legal definition in Ireland. According to the 2003 Finance Act, which gives small brewers a 50% rebate on excise duty, it is a brewery that produces less than 20,000 hectolitres of beer per annum and is 'legally and economically independent of any other brewery'.

For the purposes of this book, we define Irish craft beer as beer produced in small batches by an independent microbrewery in Ireland. Where a brewery does not meet these criteria, we make it clear in their profile in Chapter 5. In some cases they are part-owned by a large brewery or brew their beer under contract with another brewery. Being a craft producer isn't about being crafty: if a brewery is selling their beer as a craft product, we don't see why they can't be transparent about it. If you want to know your craft from your contract, check out Beoir's A to Z of Ireland's beer and cider on their website (www.beoir.org).

What's in a label?

Bottle labels contain a lot of information. They have quirky pictures, little stories about the brand and the beer, social media symbols and websites. They state how many millilitres are in the bottle, what the ABV is and what the beer is called. Sometimes, however, it can be difficult to find out where the beer actually comes from – a not unreasonable request for people who want to know that they're supporting an Irish microbrewery. The European Beer Consumers Union, which includes Beoir amongst its members, is lobbying the EU for new legislation on labelling, information and cost, and has a manifesto that states: 'Consumers have the right to know who brewed the beer and where it was brewed.' The Independent Craft Brewers of Ireland (ICBI) is moving towards implementing a mark of origin for Irish craft beer so that consumers can be assured that their beer is brewed right here in Ireland.

Terroir

Craft beers are proud of their place, or *terroir*. Loosely translated as 'a sense of place', *terroir* (a French word that means 'local') refers to the interplay of climate, soil and topography and the unique effect it has on a food or drink. It is most commonly used when talking about wine, but the concept is now gaining some traction in the beer world too, where it can be expressed in things like the wild yeast of a Belgian lambic, the fresh hops in a wet-hopped beer or even the local water the beer is brewed with.

What sets microbreweries apart from big business?

Big breweries want us – and they spend a lot of advertising money trying to persuade us – to drink their products. Go into most Irish pubs and you'll find a tap dedicated to the black one, the yellow one and the red one. No matter what pub or where it is, the same beers are on offer. They all taste the same (that is, not tasting of much), and the breweries pride themselves on that consistency. They produce a product that is designed to appeal to the broadest market possible without offending anyone's tastebuds. As Seamus O'Hara from Carlow Brewing said, 'We brew the taste in; they brew the taste out.'

Microbreweries use natural ingredients, avoid chemicals and brew in small quantities, which enables them to produce well-flavoured beers made with care and passion. These are distinctive drinks, each with their own slant on a particular style. You're not going to mix up a pint of Hilden's Twisted Hop with the Deception Golden Ale from Trouble Brewing or Whitewater Brewery's Belfast Ale – although you might have fun trying to at a beer festival! You may not like every beer – maybe it's just too hoppy for you or maybe you aren't a fan of the pronounced fruitiness in some red ales – but that's okay too. There are plenty of others to try.

One exciting feature of craft beer is that the brewers love to experiment. They all have their core range of really good, reliable, bread-and-butter beers that restaurants can print on their menus and bars can have on permanent tap. But they also have magic to play with, and some of the newer brewers have been making bold moves in this direction, launching with a ginger porter (Rascal's Brewing) or going for a black IPA as their second beer, like Blacks of Kinsale did. Small-batch brewing means a quick turnaround, so breweries can make, bottle, distribute and even run out of a beer, letting you know all the steps via social media as you race to get to the pub before the keg is drained. This is all done on slim-to-non-existent advertising budgets – sometimes a brewery's social media presence is someone at home cooking dinner while updating Facebook and Twitter with news of the brewery's latest release. There's a grass-roots energy and connection between passionate brewers and committed consumers that you would be hard pressed to find anywhere in the world of big beer.

For all the noise, microbreweries have less than 1% of the Irish beer market, but it is moving in the right direction and there's a real spirit of co-operation amongst the craft brewing community. Breweries don't just expect to convert customers to their own product – craft beer is all about broadening choice and helping consumers to be more experimental and adventurous in the beers that they try. When it comes to craft beer, a rising tide lifts all boats.

CHAPTER 2

A SHORT HISTORY OF IRISH BEER

To appreciate Irish craft beer fully, we need to go back to the very beginning – and in the beginning, there was beer.

People have been enjoying beer in one form or another for 5,000 years. It has come a long way from its sweet, gruel-like beginnings to the bitter, bubbly drink we know and love today. The earliest beer was more like porridge than a drink (picture that the next time you're having a bowl of oatmeal for breakfast), and a flavouring and preservative mixture of leaves, spices and herbs called gruit was used before hops became more common. All that might not sound very appetising, but some say that this stodgy brew was the start of civilisation.

One thing hasn't changed across the millennia, though: whether it was a group of ancient Sumerians sipping it through reed straws from a communal gourd or modern-day rounds in the pub, beer has always brought people together.

> *'He is a wise man who invented beer.' – Plato*

Beer Is the Staff of Life

They say that bread is the staff of life, but perhaps that should be beer. There is a theory that agriculture developed in order for societies to grow enough wheat and barley not so that they could bake bread, but so that they could make beer. If you follow that line of thought all the way through, you can see why some archaeologists go so far as to say that beer played a fundamental part in the formation of civilisation.

Bread and beer were staples of the diet for rich and poor alike in ancient Egypt, reflected in the fact that the hieroglyphic symbol for food was a pitcher of beer plus a loaf of bread. Even as late as the Middle Ages, beer and bread were made with the same yeast. Whichever side of the 'which came first, bread or beer?' debate you are on, it's clear that they were two sides of the same coin and were both an important part of the earliest societies.

Over the centuries, beer has always brought people together

Ale is ancient; it is one of the oldest fermented alcoholic drinks in the world. The earliest known recipe is for beer – the 4,000-year-old 'Hymn to Ninkasi', the Sumerian goddess of beer who was made to 'satisfy the desire' and 'sate the heart' and who gave divine protection to brewers. Meanwhile, the oldest set of laws, the Code of Hammurabi, dating back to 1780 BC, sets out the rations of beer to be allocated according to social standing (two litres a day for workers, five litres for priests). In ancient Egypt, beer was even used as currency – you could say that the pyramids were built on the back of beer, as the workers were paid with it. They also believed that beer had magical and medicinal powers. Doesn't it just?

> *'Do not cease to drink beer, to eat, to intoxicate thyself, to make love, and to celebrate the good days.'*
>
> *– Ancient Egyptian proverb*

A taste of history

Do you wonder what beer tasted like thousands of years ago? The brewers at Dogfish Head in Delaware did, so they got together with Dr Patrick McGovern, an expert in ancient beverages, and chemically analysed residues found in ancient vats and pottery fragments from around the world. This was then reverse-engineered to create the Ancient Ales line of beers. Some of the unusual ingredients include saffron, hawthorn fruit, annatto, pomegranates, Askinosie cocoa and Ethiopian myrrh resin. The first beer in the series, Midas Touch, which was developed based on molecular evidence from King Midas's tomb, was launched in 1999 and continues to be produced year-round. If you're ever lucky enough to spot one of these ales in an off-licence or on a trip to the US, snap it up for a taste of history.

The Middle Ages

Barley was one of the first cereal grains to be cultivated and to spread out from the Fertile Crescent, and everywhere that barley went, beer was sure to go. Mesopotamia is not only the cradle of Western civilisation – it is also the birthplace of brewing.

> *'Fermentation and civilisation are inseparable.'*
> *– John Ciardi*

Everyone from peasants to nobles drank beer, which was safer than the contaminated water common in the Middle Ages. Boiling the water killed harmful micro-organisms and the alcohol in the beer was toxic to pathogens. Hops began to be added to beer in the thirteenth century, but weren't in widespread use until the 1500s. They had been used as a medicinal plant before that, but when incorporated into beer they added an antibacterial and preservative element too.

Ale was also an important source of nutrition and calories in medieval times, with its store of vitamins, minerals, protein and antioxidants. Long before there were butter mountains and wine lakes, beer helped to bridge the gap in the lean times when food was often in short supply and spiced up a monotonous diet. Low-alcohol table beer was served at mealtimes, including breakfast, and even children drank it. Manual workers drank beer throughout the day as a source of calories and to stay hydrated. As late as the 1900s, male Guinness employees over the age of twenty-one were given a free beer allowance of two pints a day at designated taps located around the brewery, though men with physically demanding jobs were given three (the taps were closed in the 1970s, but employees still get a beer allowance to this day, which they take home in bottles). Drinking four or five litres of ale a day wasn't unheard of, though keep in mind that the alcohol content was low; it's not as if everyone was stumbling around in a drunken stupor, at least not all of the time.

Beer was used to pay fines, tolls, rents and debts, and was used as payment for workers. It was a staple part of the diet; it was used as medicine; it was an important source of calories and hydration for manual labour; it was an offering to the gods in early religious ceremonies; and weddings wouldn't have been complete without the bride-ale. Forget quinoa or broccoli or blueberries – beer was truly the first superfood.

The Era of Alewives and Brewsters

Who was doing all this brewing? From the very first brewers in Mesopotamia, Babylonia and Sumeria up until the late Middle Ages, most brewers were women. Heck, even Jane Austen brewed beer.

Remember Ninkasi? 'In almost all ancient societies, mythologies state that beer was a gift given specifically to women from a goddess (never a male god) ... who blessed their brewing vessels,' writes Pete Brown in *Man Walks into a Pub*. Women might not have had much in the Middle Ages, but the law said that those vessels remained the housewife's property. The origins of the word 'bride' are a clue as to how closely brewing and women were linked: its earliest root word, 'bru', means 'to cook, brew or make broth'. By the fifth century, the terms 'alewife' and 'brewster' were being used in England.

Brewing was part and parcel of the household chores, as common and unremarkable as baking a loaf of bread or putting a load of washing on. If women had surplus beer, they could sell it or even open taverns or alehouses, which gave them an income and independence. 'At present, we know rather little about the role of women in the early history of brewing in Ireland, save that, according to the *Chain Book of the Dublin Corporation*, which also decreed their duties, they brewed considerable volumes in Dublin in and around the fourteenth century,' writes Ian Hornsey in *A History of Beer and Brewing*.

By the sixteenth century, beer was being taken out of the hands of housewives by monks brewing beer in monasteries, and then by captains of industry. Spurred on by profit, a deeper understanding of the science behind the beer-making process and with the capital to invest in bigger and better facilities and technology, brewing moved out of the home and into commercial breweries, which could ensure better consistency in terms of quantity and quality. The widespread use of hops also played a part, since their preservative effects meant that beer could now be stored, and thus more could be made. But storage costs money and women had only a limited amount to invest. The advances ushered in by the Industrial Revolution were the final nails in the brewsters' coffin. Home brewing became a hobby rather than part of the domestic chores.

A few hundred years later, however, brewsters are back. The craft beer renaissance in the UK, the US and Ireland has seen an influx of women returning to the ancient art of brewing, whether as brewers, beer sommeliers, beer writers or interested, engaged consumers. The Campaign for Real Ale (CAMRA) reports that more than one-fifth of its members are now women, an increase of 20,000 over the past ten years. Beer is shedding the 'boys only' image it acquired over the past 100 years, and more and more women are rediscovering the pleasures of a good pint.

> *'Give me a woman who truly loves beer, and I will conquer the world.'*
> *– Kaiser Wilhelm II*

Ancient Brewing in Ireland

While all of this was happening on the Continent and in England, what was *beoir* like in Ireland? Like all northern European countries, beer has been brewed here for a very long time – since the Bronze Age, in fact. Barley was the main grain, but oats, wheat and spelt were used too, along with honey and indigenous herbs such as bog myrtle, meadowsweet, gentian and heather.

Fulachtaí fia are one of the most common types of archaeological sites in Ireland. There are about 4,500 of them around the country, although almost half of them are in Co. Cork. They are widely believed to be ancient cooking sites, but two Irish archaeologists, Declan Moore and Billy Quinn, have another theory. They say, 'We suggest that the *fulacht fiadh* was possibly multifunctional, the kitchen sink of the Bronze Age with many conceivable uses. For us, however, a primary use seems clear – these sites were Bronze Age microbreweries.'

In 2007 they carried out an experiment to see if they could in fact brew a gruit ale in a makeshift *fulacht fiadh*, and they wrote about it in detail on their website (www.mooregroup.ie). First they filled a sixty-year-old wooden trough with water, then added granite and sandstone rocks that had been heated in a fire, along with barley provided by the Galway

Hooker Brewery. They transferred it to fermentation vessels, flavoured it with elderflowers, juniper berries and yarrow, and added brewer's yeast. After only a few hours of hands-on work and three days of waiting for it to ferment, they had a 'relatively clear, copper-coloured brew with a distinctively sharp yet sweet taste … Overall, the taste was crisp, with a moderate to heavy body. In short, it was nice!'

They go on to say, 'In conclusion, beer at its most basic is fermented liquid bread and is a highly nutritious beverage. Our ancestors would have consumed ale on a daily basis as a healthy, uncontaminated comfort drink. But this does not preclude the fact that in the long Bronze Age evenings and nights, family groups likely sat around a blazing fire telling tales, interacting socially and enjoying the warmth, wellbeing and genial companionship that ale enhances.'

'Ale was an important part of Irish society,' writes beer historian and author Martyn Cornell on his blog, *Zythophile*. 'The *Crith-Gablach*, an Irish law book compiled about the middle or end of the seventh century, declared that the "seven occupations in the law of a king" were:

> Sunday, at ale drinking, for he is not a lawful *flaith* [lord] who does not distribute ale every Sunday; Monday, at legislation, for the government of the tribe; Tuesday, at *fidchell* [a popular Iron Age board game]; Wednesday, seeing greyhounds coursing; Thursday, at the pleasures of love; Friday, at horse-racing; Saturday, at judgment.

Who'd be an Irish king, eh?'

Even before the *Crith Gablach*, the *Senchus Mór*, a fifth-century tract in Ireland's Brehon laws that was compiled by St Patrick and eight others, outlines the brewing process in Ireland. It also sets out the amount of ale allowed for laymen and clerics at dinner: six pints for laymen and a measly three for clerics – the opposite of the proportion given to workers and priests in the Code of Hammurabi.

Irish ale in the Middle Ages was brown, sweet, heavy and still unhopped, and was made by women, who also ran taverns and alehouses, much as the alewives did in England. But it was also made by monks, by experts in private houses for royal or noble families (King James I is rumoured to have been a fan of Irish ale) and by professional brewers in certified, legalised alehouses. Rent could even be paid in malt or ale.

The tools for Declan Moore and Billy Quinn's experiment

Beer as Gaeilge

áith	kiln	*grúdlann*	brewery
beoir	beer	*leann*	ale
braich	malt	*ól*	ale, drink
eorna	barley	*teach*	pub
giosta	yeast	*teach braiche*	malthouse

Ale features in Irish literature, mythology and heroic tales too – it would seem that the Ulster warriors passed many hours sitting around a fire after battle drinking ale. A poem from the ninth century written for Cano Mac Gartnáin, an exiled Scottish prince who fled to Ireland, sings the praises of different kinds of Irish ale from around the country, while 'The Vision of Mac Conglinne', the famous twelfth-century parody, lists 'a vat of new ale' and 'son of beer (glory of liquors!)' in its gluttonous catalogue of food.

Irish patron saints of beer

It wasn't all just turning water into wine back in the old days – did you know that some saints are affiliated with beer?

St Brigid, patron saint of Ireland, scholars, poets, wisdom and creativity, amongst many other things, was a beer-loving woman too. Legend has it that she blessed bathwater and turned it into beer for some thirsty lepers and that she provided beer to eighteen churches for the entire Easter season, all from a single barrel from her own convent. A poem attributed to St Brigid begins, 'I should like a great lake of ale, for the King of the Kings. I should like the family of Heaven to be drinking it through time eternal.' Amen to that!

St Columbanus, an Irish missionary, is reputed to have multiplied bread and beer to feed his community, and convinced a group of pagans who were about to sacrifice a keg of beer to an idol of their god to drink it instead. He also had a clear idea of how he wanted to meet his end: 'It is my design to die in the brew-house; let ale be placed to my mouth when I am expiring, that when the choirs of angels come, they may say, "Be God propitious to this drinker."'

And let's not forget the most famous Irish saint of them all – St Patrick had a brewer in his household, a priest named Mescan.

Big Brands and the Black Stuff

Starting in the eighteenth century, the story of beer across Europe became one of industrialisation and consolidation. Developments such as steam engines, refrigeration, pasteurisation and even improvements in transport meant that beer was now being made at a commercial, not domestic, level. In fact, so much beer was being made that in the early eighteenth century, brewing was one of the most successful and prosperous industries in Dublin.

This era also witnessed the birth of brands. In Ireland, these included Murphy's, Beamish, Smithwicks and Guinness, which were eventually swallowed up by multinational behemoths such as Diageo and Heineken International. There were many other viable breweries at this time, but as in any other industry, as the big players got even bigger, the little guys simply couldn't compete and were either bought up, went under or became bottlers for their former competitors.

> *'O Beer! O Hodgson, Guinness, Allsopp, Bass!*
> *Names that should be on every infant's tongue!'*
> *– 'Beer', from* Verses and Translations *by Charles Stuart Calverley*
> *(1861)*

At the start of the nineteenth century, there were 200 breweries in Ireland[1] – fifty of them in Dublin alone. By 1850, this had more than halved to ninety-five. Fifty years later, at the start of the twentieth century, this number had plummeted to just thirty-six breweries and continued to fall steadily until 1960, 200 years after Arthur Guinness founded his brewery, when only eight remained.

---

[1] The memory of some of those early breweries is being dusted off. For example, Dublin's J.W. Sweetman brewpub is a nod to the original eighteenth-century Sweetmans, which had five breweries in the capital, while the Wm Cairnes gastropub in Drogheda, Co. Louth, is built on the site of the old Cairnes Brewery, which was in operation for 150 years, and even exported its bottled stout to the US.

Number of breweries in Ireland

1832: 216	**1925:** 20
1840: 191	**1930:** 16
1850: 95	**1940:** 14
1900: 36	**1955:** 13
1905: 31	**1960:** 8
1915: 25	**2014:** 46

You can't talk about beer in Ireland without talking about Guinness. The iconic stout is perhaps the country's most famous export, up there with Bono and Kerrygold butter. The Guinness Storehouse in Dublin consistently ranks as the number one tourist attraction in the country – Queen Elizabeth even visited during her state visit of 2011, although she only stared at the pint that was poured for her and didn't have a taste. No celebrity can visit Ireland without a pint of the black stuff being thrust into their hand. When it comes to beer, Ireland is synonymous with stout.

Arthur Guinness founded his brewery at St James's Gate along the River Liffey in 1759. He brewed ales initially, introducing his first porter in 1778. In 1799 he decided to focus solely on porter, and the recipe remained unchanged for almost 200 years, all the way up to 1973. Guinness was the first big brewery to float shares on the stock market and the first brewery to run a modern-day ad campaign. By the early twentieth century, Guinness was the largest brewery in the world and Arthur's eponymous stout was being sold all over the globe. Today, 10 million pints of Guinness are downed every day in 150 countries. That kind of clout means that Guinness has had a big effect on brewing in Ireland, both in terms of the brewing industry itself and on our palates.

The Beamish & Crawford and Murphy's breweries, which were both brewers of stout located in Cork, gave Guinness a good run for their money for a while in the nineteenth century. By the early 1800s Beamish & Crawford was the biggest brewery in what was then the UK, and Murphy's was no slouch either. By 1900, however, the tables had turned and Guinness was the biggest brewery in all of Europe. Murphy's went into bankruptcy in 1982 and was taken over by Heineken a year later. The Beamish & Crawford Brewery was closed in 2009, since Heineken eventually came to own that brewery as well and didn't need two breweries in one city. Even Smithwicks, which celebrated its 300th birthday in 2010 and is now owned by Diageo, closed its historic brewery in Kilkenny in 2013 and turned it into a visitor centre.

A tale of two stouts: Cork vs. Dublin

The rivalry between Cork and Dublin stouts goes back a long way. It's not just a matter of geography or the GAA – there's also a noticeable difference in their taste. If you compare them side by side, you'll notice that Beamish and Murphy's are more chocolatey than Guinness, which has a more prominent metallic tang and roasted barley flavour. Unlike most dry stouts, which tend to have little hop aroma, Cork stout also has a notable floral bouquet.

Guinness has also had a huge influence on the taste of a nation. Through their economies of scale, their clever use of new transport systems, their network of national agents and by undercutting their competition to gain market share, Guinness was available all over Ireland by the early 1900s. It was so ubiquitous and successful that it practically sold itself – Guinness didn't even advertise in Ireland or England until the late 1920s, when the famous 'Guinness is good for you' campaign was launched.

Porter was born in London in the early 1700s, when it was simply called brown beer. Irish brewers put their own stamp on the style when they developed the signature Irish dry stout – *leann dubh*, or 'black beer' – and soon we were exporting huge amounts of it to England rather than the other way around. By 1846, Irish porter was said to be better than London porter. Made with roasted unmalted barley, it was originally brewed this way to save a few bob on duty after a tax on malt was introduced in 1786. Porter was first brewed in Ireland in 1776, and by the 1900s Irish dry stout had become the most popular beer style here. Stout remained Ireland's favourite beer for the next 100 years – the only country where this was the case – until lager finally stole its crown in 1999. Today, lager has 60% of the market, stout 35% and ale 5%, although Guinness remains the best-selling brand and accounts for one in every three pints sold in pubs. Britain eventually embraced pale ale after porter's working-class heyday in the 1800s, while Europe and the US prefer lager. Ireland, though, has made stout all its own.

Porter and ale in Ireland: A case of city mouse, country mouse

'Prior to 1850, the market for beer was limited to towns and cities, due to the countryside being essentially a subsistence economy with a taste for poitín – which had a higher alcohol content than beer, and was cheaper to make on a small scale. The big city brewers were chiefly making porter, due to the size of their market and the economies of scale associated with porter brewing, while the brewers in the small country towns generally concentrated on ales.' – Iorwerth Griffiths, *Beer and Cider in Ireland: The Complete Guide* (2007)

The consolidation that took place in Ireland in the nineteenth and twentieth centuries mirrors what happened in the UK and the US. The UK had around 350 breweries when CAMRA was founded in 1971. While this might sound like a lot at first, it represented a huge drop from the 3,556 breweries in existence in 1915. By the 1970s, only forty breweries were left in the US. Happily, those numbers have dramatically reversed: as of 2013, there were nearly 1,150 microbreweries in the UK, a seventy-year high, and almost 2,800 in the US, up from a mere eight craft breweries in 1980, with a further 1,700 breweries in the planning stages.

The relentless march of globalisation means that 85% of all beer sold in Ireland today comes from five mega umbrella brands: C&C Group, Diageo, Heineken, Molson Coors and SABMiller. We have come a long way from the days when every town and city had its own brewery making local beer for local people.

The macro Irish brewers aren't even Irish any more, but the big brands are big business. According to the Irish Brewers Association and a 2013 report by Ernst & Young, the Irish beer industry:

- Employs 1,500 people directly in brewing companies and indirectly supports 40,800 jobs as well as 4,000 farming jobs (as of 2012).
- Contributes €1.2 billion to the exchequer and €1.3 billion in added value to the Irish economy.
- Produces over 800 million litres of beer every year, 76.8 million of which are exported.
- Spends €400 million purchasing goods and services in Ireland on everything from transport to agricultural products.

Even so, the homogenous globalisation and dumbing down of beer is proving to be its own undoing, as the lack of diversity has created an opening in the market. As people travelled abroad and tasted the characterful real ales in the UK or the hoppy IPAs in the US, they came home with more adventurous palates, wanting something more – more variety, more choice, more taste.

Cue craft beer.

The Craft Beer Revolution

Craft beer has become the poster child of the Irish economy, a good news story of success, innovation and entrepreneurship, even in the middle of a biting recession. Sales of craft beer in Ireland increased by 35% in 2013 when compared to 2012, and jumped by 42.5% from 2011 to 2012. When craft brewers were polled in 2013, 80% said that they expected to expand significantly over the next three years.

The picture wasn't always so positive: most of the early Irish micro-brewery efforts in the 1990s were before their time and proved to be short-lived. For such a famously beer-loving nation – half of all alcohol sold in Ireland is beer and we consistently rank among the top beer-consuming nations in the world – it is curious that we lagged so far behind the US and the UK, whose craft beer revivals started in the 1970s and 1980s. We are making up for lost time now though.

Following a 200-year process of industrialisation, globalisation and consolidation, the pendulum is swinging back. Beer sales are falling overall in Ireland, the UK and the US, but sales of craft beer are way up. This hasn't gone unnoticed by the big brands. Seeing their own sales slipping, they are getting in on the craft act, brewing their own craft-style beers (think Blue Moon wheat beer from the US), slapping the word 'craft' on their own mass-produced spin-offs or buying up microbreweries. The first such buyout in Ireland occurred in 2013, when Molson Coors added the Franciscan Well to their craft beer stable.

The irony of the craft beer revolution is that rather than blazing a new trail, it's actually a throwback to the past, when there were hundreds of breweries around the country and beer was a local product. Yet craft brewers *are* trailblazers in the way they innovate, experiment, play with flavours and just plain have fun. Unlike, say, European cheese-makers, who tend to be bound by strict traditions going back generations, craft brewers respect the past but aren't tied to it. Where would be the fun in that?

Craft beer by the numbers

- **60:** The total number of breweries and contract brewers that are in production in Ireland as of summer 2014: 44 craft breweries, 14 contract brewers and 2 multinationals.

- **80:** The percentage of craft beer producers who expect to expand significantly over the period 2013 to 2016.

- **42.5:** The percentage increase in sales of craft beer in 2012 compared to 2011.

- **35:** The percentage increase in sales in 2013 compared to 2012.

- **7:** Microbreweries employ seven times more people per hectolitre compared to the multinationals.

- **0.5:** The percentage of the Irish beer market that craft beer currently accounts for.

- **1,150:** The number of microbreweries in the UK as of 2013.

- **2,700:** The number of microbreweries in the US as of 2013, with a further 1,700 in planning stages.

Don't drink beer from strangers – support your local brewery

Where to Next?

Craft beer accounts for less than 1% of the Irish beer market (it's 8% in the US and 2% in the UK), so the only way to go is up. For comparison's sake, if the US had the same number of breweries per capita as Germany, they would have about 5,000 breweries. Denver, Colorado, which is a little bigger than Dublin, has around fifty craft breweries, so why couldn't our capital city be home to a similar number? After all, when Arthur Guinness set up shop there were over sixty breweries in Dublin alone, and there were six breweries and eight distilleries in Cork in the nineteenth century.

Irish producers themselves believe that craft beer and cider could have 5% of the market by 2016. An even more ambitious prediction from *Hospitality Ireland* says that craft beer is expected to grow from the current €24 million to €235 million in retail sales value, or 10% of the Irish beer market, by 2017. In the US, there are predictions that craft beer sales could triple by 2019. Meanwhile, many Irish craft brewers are struggling to keep up as demand sometimes outstrips supply, and are trying to increase their capacity as quickly as possible.

Some say that the popularity of craft beer is just a passing fad. While it is inevitable that this growth will eventually level off, these are hardly the signs of a tapped-out trend. A new world of flavours and choice has been opened up and we're not going back.

Ireland has one of the highest rates of per capita beer consumption in the world, consistently ranking in the top five or top ten nations. Imagine what that kind of purchasing power could do for the craft beer industry if it became less of a niche product and more mainstream. Billionaire Dr Pearse Lyons of Alltech believes that Ireland could even become the 'epicentre of craft brewing and distilling', saying that 'Ireland, with its rich history in brewing … is the perfect place to build on this craft brewing revolution'.

Viva la revolution? We'll drink to that.

> *'I have a total irreverence for anything connected with society except that which makes the roads safer, the beer stronger, the food cheaper and the old men and old women warmer in the winter and happier in the summer.'*
>
> *– Brendan Behan*

CHAPTER 3

SAVOURING BEER

Top Tips for Tasting Beer

The glass

The right glass for the right beer will let you fully appreciate all it has to offer in terms of its appearance, aroma, taste and texture. See pages 56–63 for more.

The pour

First, pour it properly! There's nothing worse than getting a glass of suds and having to wait for what seems like an eternity for it to settle. Take a moment at the start to concentrate. The glass needs to be tilted at 45° while you pour the beer down the side. When the glass is half full, turn it up straight and pour the rest of the beer into the centre. With bottle-conditioned beer, there may be some yeast sediment (and B vitamins!) in the bottom of the bottle. Drink or not? It's up to you.

The look

We eat, and drink, with our eyes first, so with your glass of beer in hand, take a good look at it. Is the colour brown, light gold or as dark as the ace of spades? What is the clarity like? Clear and sparkling or appropriately hazy? For example, unfiltered wheat beers will have a distinctive cloudy appearance. Does it have a foamy head or something that disperses in moments? As you drink, you might notice lacing, the foam that clings to the sides of a beer glass as the level goes down. Also, take note of the carbonation: are there lots of bubbles or just a few strays?

The aroma

Give the glass a careful swirl – you don't want to spill half the beer down your front – and just like you do with wine, put your nose into the glass and inhale. Smell and taste are inextricably linked, and this will give you an idea of what to expect when you taste it. Of course, if your beer is too cold you won't be able to smell or taste much at all, so don't over-chill it.

Malt is the main ingredient in beer, and you may be able to pick out its toasty, biscuity, caramel flavours, perhaps even espresso or chocolate aromas from roasted barley. Hops contribute their own distinctive and aromatic layers of herbs, flowers, citrus or pine. Ale yeasts bring fruity esters to the party, along the lines of raisins, bananas and butterscotch. Are you getting a whiff of alcohol or of special ingredients like vanilla, ginger or chilli? If it is a barrel-aged beer, it can pick up a lot of character from the wood or the previous inhabitants of the barrel.

Roll out the barrel

In a world of stainless steel, craft beer is playing a role in keeping the once-endangered art of the cooper alive. After fermentation, beer can be stored in pre-used barrels for a period of time, letting it absorb flavour from the wood and from whatever beverage was in the barrel previously. Naturally enough, oak whiskey barrels are particularly popular in Ireland, while bourbon barrels are often used in the US. Paul McLaughlin of Kelvin Cooperage says that brewers are also using new oak barrels, some with internal toasting or charring, and old wine barrels.

The taste

Ahhhh, the first sip. Was it worth waiting for? Be sure to swallow it slowly! Are you getting flavour confirmation of those aromas you were picking up? Hop flavours, which can vary from mild to pronounced, are similar to aroma, so we are back to using terms like citrus, fruit, flowers, grass, pine, wood, pepper and spice. The hops should have a distinctive refreshing bitterness to balance out the malt sweetness. The intense espresso bitterness of roasted barley will do something similar. Does it feel balanced, with no one element dominating the other?

The texture

This is the all-important mouthfeel. Take a second sip and consider. How much is the beer carbonated? What kind of body does it have – light, medium, full? Does it have a clean, crisp consistency, is it rich and oily, or is it a little bit thin, even watery?

The aftertaste

Also known as finish, this is the taste that lingers in your mouth after you eat or drink something. Enthusiasts consider the finish to be an important aspect of a beer overall, just like it is with wine. What kinds of flavours linger? Is there a refreshing hop bitterness, often experienced as an aftertaste at the back of the tongue? Some beers have a harshly bitter finish, while others have no aftertaste whatsoever – ideally, it will be pleasant and balanced. Different styles of beer will have correspondingly different aftertastes, from the crisp, clean finish of a lager to the dry, lightly astringent aftertaste of roasted barley in a stout. Most importantly of all, does the beer have the drinkability factor that begs for another sip?

> *'No beer truly tastes the same at the brewery as it does in a pub suffused by the warmth of friends and the smells of perfume and food. Nor will a beer taste the same on a fishing boat as it does in front of a fireplace. Some parts of beer flavour will be measureable and others will not. For those of us who do not analyse beer for a living, perhaps any analysis of beer flavour should largely be a matter of personal enjoyment and the provision of good hospitality.'*
> *– Garrett Oliver,* The Oxford Companion to Beer *(2012)*

Beer Tasting Terms Cheat Sheet

Colour

pale straw	deep gold	deep amber	ruby brown
straw	pale amber	amber brown	deep brown
pale gold	medium amber	brown	black

Appearance and clarity

bright	cloudy	inky	sparkling
clear	hazy	opaque	turbid

Head

creamy	fine	large	persistent
delicate	fluffy	lingering	pillowy
dense	foamy	long-lasting	rocky
dissipates	frothy	loose	tightly knit
quickly	lacy	moussy	

Aroma (hops)

cedar	grassy	nutty	sawdust
citrus	hay	orange	spicy
earthy	herbal	pear	spruce
eucalyptus	lemon	perfume	straw
floral	lime	pine	tropical fruit
fruity	melon	resinous	woody
grapefruit	minty	roses	

Aroma (malt)

biscuit	cereal	espresso	raisin
bread	coffee	fig	smoky
brown sugar	corn	grain	toast
burnt sugar	currants	nutty	toffee
caramel	dark chocolate	prune	treacle

Fruit flavours

apple	dates	melon	plum
banana	grapefruit	orange	prune
blackberry	jam	passionfruit	raisin
blackcurrant	lemon	peach	raspberry
coconut	lime	pear	strawberry
currants	lychee	pineapple	

Floral flavours

elderflower	grass	herbal	nettle
geranium	hay	marigold	rose

Roasted flavours

biscuit	coffee	malt	toast
bread	cracker	oatmeal	woody
brown sugar	espresso	roasted barley	yeasty
burnt	grain	smoky	

Spice flavours

allspice	clove	lemongrass	pepper
chilli	coriander	nutmeg	vanilla
cinnamon	herbal	orange peel	

Sweet flavours

brown sugar	caramel	honey	toffee
bubblegum	chocolate	jam	vanilla
butterscotch	golden syrup	liquorice	

Alcohol (ethanol) flavours

boozy	harsh	peat	vodka
bourbon	honey	port	whiskey
brandy	Madeira	rum	wine
cider	musty	sherry	
esters	oak	solvents	

'Off' flavours and aromas

alcoholic	cooked onion	leathery	rancid
almond	cooked	meaty	rotten eggs
barnyard	sweetcorn	medicinal	rotten
boozy	cooked tomato	metallic	vegetables
burnt rubber	damp earth	mouldy	rubbery
buttered	dirt	musty	skunky
popcorn	garlic	nail polish	soapy
butterscotch	goaty	remover	solvents
cabbage	grass	oil	sour milk
cardboard	greasy	oxidised	stale
catty	green apples	paper	sulphuric
celery	heavy	parsnip	tar
cheese	hollow	phenolic	turpentine
chemical	horsey	plastic	vinegar

Mouthfeel

aggressive	dusty	mouth-coating	spicy
alkaline	effervescent	oily	spritzy
astringent	flat (under-	powdery	stale
bitter	carbonated)	refreshing	sticky
chalky	full-bodied	robust	sweet
chewy	gassy (over-	round	syrupy
clean	carbonated)	salty	tart
cloying	grainy	sharp	thick/viscous
creamy	gritty	silky	thin/watery
crisp	heavy	smooth	vinous/winey
delicate	light	soft	warming
drying	metallic	sour	weak

Chalice/goblet   Flute   IPA

Snifter   Stange

What's in a Glass?

Beer writer Michael Jackson said, 'So popular is beer, the world's best-selling alcoholic drink, that it is often taken for granted. Yet scientific analysis shows that a glass of beer has within it as many aromas and flavours as fine wine.' You wouldn't swill a top-class wine straight from the bottle, so why wouldn't you treat a craft beer with the same respect? Sure, it's part of beer's casual charm to be able to stand around in the pub or the back garden necking it straight from the bottle without bothering about glasses or worrying about breaking your stemware, but you're doing your beer a disservice.

- **Appearance:** A glass lets you appreciate the colour and shows off the head on a beer, which is not only visually appealing but also adds a textural contrast and is crucial where aromas are concerned.
- **Aroma:** Just as you swirl wine around in a wine glass to release the bouquet, swirling beer in a glass unlocks the volatiles, which is a fancy way of saying the things that make beer smell, such as hop oils and esters. The popular tulip glass is particularly good at concentrating aroma.

Mug   Pilsner   Pint

Tulip   Weizen   Wine

- **Taste:** Appearance, aroma and texture are all well and good, but flavour is king. A glass makes the most of a beer's flavour by allowing all four components to show off their full potential. You lose all that when you drink beer straight from the bottle.
- **Texture:** The simple act of pouring a beer into a glass allows the carbonation to come out and play and is what forms the head, which in turn helps to trap some of the aromas. The specific shape of the glass accommodates how the head of the beer is formed – think of the huge foamy head on a wheat beer and how the typical weizen glass is tall enough to hold it in without it spilling over the sides. Nucleated glasses help to keep up a steady stream of bubbles and preserve the head; without those etchings and pits in the bottom of the glass, the head of a beer can go flat in just a few minutes.

Your glass should have no traces of oil or soap, which will ruin the delicate head and lacing on a beer.

What is a growler?

A recent arrival on the Irish craft beer scene, these large, reusable bottles have long been used in the US, Australia and New Zealand. Typically, growlers are filled directly from the bar tap and sealed with a swing top to keep the beer fresh for a few days. It is a perfect way to take home some good beer for sharing. We are not going to mention what the term is slang for, but we will tell you that you can get beer growlers in J.W. Sweetman and L. Mulligan Grocers in Dublin as well as The Bierhaus in Cork.

Chalice and goblet

Chalices and goblets are interchangeable, but if you want to split hairs, a goblet is thinner and more delicate than the thicker, sturdier chalice. The short, thick stem and wide-mouthed, bowl-shaped glass are perfect for big sips of bold beers with plenty of aroma and flavour. As such, they are designed to keep the beer's head intact. Think heavy-hitting Trappist brews like Chimay in its well-known branded goblet.

Use with: Belgian ales, strong ales, farmhouse ales, bocks, dubbels, tripels, barrel-aged beers, kriek or framboise

Flute

Flutes aren't just for champagne. Their long, thin shape concentrates aroma and shows off the sparkle of a highly carbonated beer or even cider, which is a nod to cider's refined past, when it was served in decorative flutes.

Use with: Pilsners, Belgian lambics (such as gueuze), fruit beers, krieks, wild ales and cider

IPA

Launched in 2013 after two years of research, the IPA glass is a brand new arrival on the glassware scene. The result of a collaboration between American brewers Sam Calagione of Dogfish Head, Ken Grossman of Sierra Nevada and the Bavarian glassmaker Spiegelau, this is the first glass designed specifically to showcase India pale ales.

Use with: India pale ales primarily, but any other particularly aromatic beer, such as a Belgian ale, pale ale or stout, could work well in this glass too

In February 2014, Spiegelau unveiled a brand new stout glass that looks like a cross between a tulip glass and a stange. They say that it 'accentuates the roasted malt, rich coffee and chocolate notes that define the stout beer style'.

Mug, stein and tankard

These are the ye olde option of the beer glassware world – think hefty steins in German beer halls or dimpled mugs in traditional English real ale pubs. The main difference between a mug and a stein is the hinged lid on a stein, which some say was introduced during the Black Plague to keep diseased fleas or bugs out of the beer. Made for plenty of convivial clinking, these are easy and fun to drink out of.

Use with: Ales (especially cask ales), lagers, bitters, bocks, stouts and porters

Pilsner and pokal

A pilsner glass has a long, slender, trumpet-like design, but no stem. The pokal has a similar shape as a pilsner glass, but it does have a stem. Both are designed to showcase a pilsner's golden sparkle and creamy, pillowy head.

Use with: Pilsners, lagers, bocks and doppelbocks

Pint

The most ubiquitous glass is also the least popular amongst beer aficionados. Pint glasses are functional and practical for pubs and restaurants because they can be stacked, but they don't do very much for the beer itself. Good glassware accentuates the beer's aroma and the head, but a pint glass doesn't really do either. What it does do is release carbonation at a consistent rate, which is good for beer styles that are meant to have less carbonation anyway, such as porters, stouts, brown ales and cask ales.

A pint means different things in different places – the imperial glass used in Irish and British pubs holds 570ml (20 fl oz), while the shaker pint in the US holds 450ml (16 fl oz). There are many different types of pint glasses: imperial, nonic, Prague, shaker, Tokyo and tulip.

Use with: This glass doesn't discriminate. It can be – and is – used for any beer.

1 imperial pint = 570ml (20 fl oz)

1 American pint = 450ml (16 fl oz)

Snifter

More commonly used for brandy or cognac, a snifter is all about the aroma. The generous balloon-shaped glass leaves plenty of room for swirling the beer, which releases the volatiles, and the shape invites you to cup it in your hand, which helps to warm up the beer slightly. A good choice for any strong beer.

Use with: Imperial stouts, barley wines, barrel-aged beers, quadrupels, double IPAs or strong ales

Stange

Stange means 'stick' or 'rod' in German, which is appropriate given the slim, straight-sided design of this glass, which has traditionally been used for German kölsch beers or, increasingly, any delicate beer. Its small shape helps to keep the beer cold and refreshing and maintains the carbonation. A collins glass is a good substitute for a stange, or even a highball in a pinch.

Use with: Kölsch, lagers, golden ales

A flight of beer

A gaggle of geese, a school of fish – and a flight of beer. A beer flight is the name given to a sampling of different beers, usually four to six, which should be tasted in order from lightest to darkest. Or you could try different versions of the same beer style, such as a few different varieties of ales or stouts. You're likely to be served a flight of beer on specially designed wooden paddles in a brewpub, though they might also be served on a pre-printed placemat that includes tasting notes for each beer.

Tulip

The Nigella Lawson of glassware, the evocative curves of a tulip glass capture the aroma and the pouty lip holds in the head, so this is a good glass for strong, malty, aromatic ales. Holding the glass by the stem also means that the beer doesn't warm up in your hand.

Use with: Lagers, Scottish ales, Belgian ales, double or imperial IPAs, barley wines and other aromatic beers that pack a punch

Weizen

This tall glass was designed to accommodate the famously frothy head on a wheat beer, while the shape helps to concentrate the trademark banana and clove flavours and aromas.

Use with: Wheat beers

That innocent-looking lemon wedge that's often served with wheat beers is actually quite controversial. Purists say that the trademark banana and clove flavours of a good wheat beer don't need a squeeze of lemon to distract from them. But even more to the point, the citric acid kills the huge head that wheat beers are famous for.

Wine glass

You might not have any specialist beer glassware, but chances are you at least have a few wine glasses knocking around. If all else fails, try serving your beer in these.

Use with: Serve pilsners, wheat beers or any light beer in white wine glasses and stronger, darker beers in red wine glasses. Serve Belgian ales in oversized (22 fl oz) wine glasses.

Beer Glassware Cheat Sheet

Glass	Use With
Chalice, goblet	Belgian ales, strong ales, farmhouse ales, bocks, dubbels, tripels, barrel-aged beers, kriek or framboise
Flute	Pilsners, Belgian lambics (such as gueuze), fruit beers, krieks, wild ales, cider
IPA	Designed specifically for India pale ales, but any other particularly aromatic beer, such as a Belgian ale, pale ale or stout, could work well in this glass too
Mug, stein, tankard	Ales (especially cask ales), lagers, bitters, bocks, stouts, porters
Pilsner, pokal	Pilsners, lagers, bocks, doppelbocks
Pint	Any beer
Snifter	Imperial stouts, barley wines, barrel-aged beers, quadrupels, double IPAs, strong ales
Stange	Kölsch, lagers, golden ales
Taster	Any beer you want to sample
Tulip	Lagers, Scottish ales, Belgian ales, double or imperial IPAs, barley wines
Weizen	Wheat beers
Wine glass	Serve pilsners, wheat beers or any light beer in white wine glasses; stronger, darker beers in red wine glasses; and Belgian ales in oversized (22 fl oz) wine glasses

Don't forget to read page 51 for tips on how to pour the perfect pint.

Serving Temperatures

Temperature makes a big difference to your beer. Here are a few rules of thumb to keep in mind.

- Cold kills flavour. Don't serve beer ice-cold unless you don't actually want to taste it.
- Ales and beers with a higher ABV tend to favour a warmer temperature, which allows their fruity notes to come out.
- Lighter, less alcoholic beers (such as lagers) are best served at a cooler temperature to keep them crisp and refreshing.
- Ideal temperatures vary, but lightly chilled (in the range of 6–13°C/42–55°F) will do at a pinch for most beers.

Ice-cold (0–4°C/32–39°F): Mass-produced beers that you have no interest in actually tasting – cold temperatures kill flavour

Well chilled – refrigerator temperature (5–8°C/41–46°F): Blonde ale, fruit beers, IPAs, kölsch, lager, pale ale, pilsner, wheat beer

Cool (7–9°C/45–48°F): Bock and doppelbock, brown ale, darker lager, lambics, pale abbey-style beer, red ale, saison and other farmhouse ales

Moderate (9–11°C/48–52°F): Darker and strong ales, dubbel, golden ale, porter, stout, tripel

Cellar temperature (11–13°C/52–55°F): Barley wine, barrel-aged beer, bitter and ESB, cask ale, imperial stout, Scotch ales

> If you've ever stashed a few steins in the freezer, don't! Frozen glasses can create ice crystals in beer or dilute it with condensation, not to mention kill the flavour because the beer is too cold. Frost can also absorb flavours from the freezer, and you don't want those in your beer. Chill the beer, not the glass.

Storing Beer

Unlike wine, which can improve and become more valuable with age, most beer is meant to be consumed right away. There are exceptions, of course – barley wines, imperial stouts, strong ales, lambics and wild ales can all benefit from being left to mature – but most beer has a short shelf life before it starts to take a turn for the worse. That said, you can generally store beer for a few months without it coming to any harm. If you want to create a beer cellar, that's a whole other story. Here are a few pointers if you're just looking to stash some beer away for a few weeks.

- Like the Traveling Wilburys' song says, store it in a cool, dry place.
- Keeping the beer in a dark place, out of direct sunlight, is crucial to avoid light strike, which can make your beer develop skunky flavours or aromas.
- Store beer upright (though if space is tight in your fridge, go ahead and store it on its side for a little while). There is a school of thought that says any beer with a cork in it should be stored on its side, like wine, but modern corks tend not to dry out, thus rendering that argument moot. Prolonged exposure to the cork can impart the flavour of the cork to the beer if the bottle is stored on its side. Storing beer upright is particularly important for bottle-conditioned beers in order to keep the yeasty sediment at the bottom of the bottle, where it belongs.
- Storing beer at the right temperature is key. Too warm, and the beer will go stale. Too cold, and the beer could turn cloudy or might not mature properly, if that's what you're aiming for. A constant cellar temperature of 10–13°C (50–55°F) is your best bet.
- Strong beers with a high alcohol content (over 7%), such as barley wines, tripels or strong ales, tend to store and age better than lighter, less alcoholic beers, which are best enjoyed fresh.
- Check the use-by date on the bottle. There's usually no point storing beer past this time.

CHAPTER 4

CIDER HOUSE RULES

A Short History of Cider in Ireland

Apples have been grown in Ireland for at least 3,000 years. They feature in the Ulster legends and are mentioned in Irish literature as far back as the seventh century. St Patrick is even said to have planted a number of apple trees in Ireland – not exactly an Irish Johnny Appleseed, but still an indication of apples' importance all the same. It seems logical to assume that people have been making cider in one form or another for much of that time.

There are plenty of early references to apples in Ireland. 'No other tree appears so frequently as the apple in early Irish documents. Apples appear in the sagas, in the voyages, in place-name lore, in the lives of the saints and in the Fenian tales. Records of apples appear in the annals,' write Lamb and Hayes in *The Irish Apple: History and Myth*. Despite the lack of written sources regarding the early history of making cider in Ireland, we know that Ireland has a rich heritage of cider-making, especially in Co. Armagh, aka the Orchard County, with its 6,000 acres of apple trees, as well as in Dublin, Kilkenny, Limerick, Waterford, Cork and south Tipperary.

Apples in the early days

Barley is one of the oldest cultivated grains and apples are the oldest cultivated fruit, so it is no surprise that beer and cider are two of the oldest fermented drinks. The native European crab apple, *Malus sylvestris* ('forest apple'), has been growing wild since Neolithic times – remains of crab apples found at Mount Sandel in Co. Derry show that Stone Age hunter-gatherers were eating this native wild apple 9,000 years ago. When Julius Caesar's soldiers began their conquest of Britain around 55 BC, they found the people there making cider, presumably from crab apples.

Early Irish law (Brehon law) outlined the brewing process at the time, but it also dealt with certain types of trees and shrubs that were important to the lives of the people in the seventh and eighth centuries. The Old Irish *crann aball*, or crab apple tree, is among the seven *airig fedo*, 'nobles of the wood', which were protected (the others being ash, hazel, holly, oak, Scots pine and yew). The bark of the crab apple tree was used to dye wool red or yellow, its wood makes a good fuel and it was valued for its fruit too, not least for making an ancient kind of cider called *nenadmin*. Even now, bitter, highly tannic cider apples are more closely related to wild crab apples than to eating or cooking apples. These days, wild Irish crab apples grow in woods, scrubland and hedgerows. Too sour to be eaten raw, they have traditionally been made into wine, verjuice, jelly and, of course, cider.

> 'Cider and apple wine are traditional. You will need about 12kg of crab apples to give 5 litres of juice. The apples should be left on the trees as long as possible but not exposed to hard frosts. Then they should be shaped into a heap and allowed to mature for a few weeks in a shady frost-free place, before crushing or pressing.'
> – Biddy White Lennon and Evan Doyle, Wild Food *(2013)*

One of the earliest documented references to cider in Ireland dates back to 1155, when the chieftain Macan (McCann) was praised for his strong cider, made from apples in his own orchards in what is now the apple-growing area of Ulster. Evidence of cider-making has also been found in monastic settlements, which were vital for keeping the tradition and knowledge of cider-making alive during the Dark Ages. The Irish Seed Savers Association, University College Dublin and the Armagh Orchards Trust in Northern Ireland have even rescued a medieval cider apple called Caledon that was developed by the monks at Tynan Abbey near Killylea in Co. Armagh.

We might also have the English to thank for our long-standing love of cider, as the plantations in the sixteenth and seventeenth centuries saw the establishment of many orchards around Ireland. For example, Edward Wakefield's 1812 account of the rural economy states: 'The first plantations of fruit trees in Waterford were in a great measure owing to the industry of the English brought over and settled hereabouts, by the first Earl of Cork ... it is said, that the first cider made in this country was at Affane, by one Greatrakes, who came over upon the settlement of Munster.' So great was the English love of cider by this time that the seventeenth century was dubbed 'the Golden Age of apples' in England. William of Orange is even believed to have sent his cider-maker, Paul le Harper, to Portadown in advance of the Battle of the Boyne in 1690 to make cider for the troops.

In *The Country Cooking of Ireland*, Colman Andrews says that the Irish 'almost certainly made cider from the juice of crab apples before the advent of large-scale apple cultivation, and once the Anglo-Normans began planting apple orchards around the island, cider-making became common. By the seventeenth century, it had turned into a major agricultural occupation – especially in areas with large English populations, like the northern counties and Cork, Limerick, Wexford and Waterford in the south. Margaret Johnson, an American authority on Irish food, calls that era "the First Golden Age of Cider" and reports that more than 250 named varieties of cider apples were cultivated in Ireland at the time.' Think about that for a second – that's 250 *cider* apples, not to mention eating or cooking apples. In her book *Ingenious Ireland*, Mary Mulvihill writes that 'at one time, over 1,000 varieties of apples were grown in these islands, differing in characteristics such as colour, taste, flowering season and keeping quality'.

The prevalence of Irish place names that have *úll* ('apple') in them are a clue as to how common orchards once were around the country.

Aghowle, Co. Wicklow (from *Achadhadhla*, 'the field of the apple trees')

Ballyhooly, Co. Cork (from *Baile Átha hÚlla*, 'pass of the ford of the apple trees')

Cappaghnanool, Co. Galway (from *Ceapach na n-ubhal*, 'plot of the apples')

Clonoulty, Co. Tipperary (from *Cluain Ul*a, 'meadow of the apple trees')

Oola, Co. Limerick (from *Úlla*, 'apple')

Oulart, Co. Wexford (from *An tAbhallort*, 'the orchard')

As with so many other foods, that diversity and heritage slowly disappeared over the years. In the early 1990s, the Irish Seed Savers Association started to search for the last surviving Irish apple varieties. Working with the Armagh Orchards Trust, they have found over 140 different types of native Irish apple trees, all of which are now growing in their orchards in Co. Clare, as well as at a sister site at University College Dublin to form the National Apple Collection, with such evocative names as Blood of the Boyne, Cavan Honeycomb or Irish Peach. If you're interested in buying a heritage apple tree, check out the Irish Seed Savers Association catalogue (www.irishseedsavers.ie).

Mentions of Irish cider are a bit easier to come by after the eighteenth century. The Dublin Society, founded in 1731, offered prizes for members who made the best cider (and, interestingly, the best beer brewed with Irish hops). In the early 1800s, a cider made in Cork by a Mr Drew was so superior that the Society judges thought it must have been mixed with foreign wine. Records from the 1800s note the excellent quality of Irish cider from demesnes and farmhouse orchards around the country. Edward Wakefield's *An Account of Ireland from 1812* says that apples from Kilkenny were famed for their quality, while *The Farmer's Magazine* from 1863 notes that good-quality cider was made in Waterford and Cork.

Irish apple varieties

Ahern Beauty	Finola Lee
Antrim Strawberry	Glenstal Cooker
Ard Cairn Russet	Irish Molly
Ballinora Pippin	Irish Peach
Ballyfatten	Irish Pitcher
Ballyvaughan Seedling	Irish Russet
Beauty of Ballintaylor	Keegan's Crab
Blood of the Boyne	Kerry Pippin
Cavan Cabbage Stalk	Kilkenny Pearmain
Cavan Honeycomb	Kiltoghert Blossom
Cavan Rose	Lady's Finger of Offaly
Cavan Strawberry	Leitrim Red
Cavan Sugarcane	Lough Key Crab
Cavan Wine	Lough Tree of Wexford
Cockagee	Munster Tulip

Many descriptions of Irish cider in the 1800s go hand in hand with mentions of the Cockagee apple, which was renowned for making excellent cider (despite its rather unfortunate name: the Anglicised word 'Cockagee' appears to come from the Irish *cac a' ghé*, 'goose shit', perhaps due to the appearance of the pulped apples or their yellow-green colour). As far back as the 1770s, Arthur Young visited Co. Clare and noted in his *Tour in Ireland*, 'This country is famous for cyder-orchards, the cakagee especially, which is incomparably fine', while Wakefield's *An Account of Ireland* also notes that the Cockagee cider from Clare was 'highly extolled, and held in great estimation' as well as being 'celebrated for its extraordinary flavour'. A few years later, in 1815, Charles Smith wrote that 'the Burlington crab, or earl of Cork's pippin, and an harsh austere apple, called the Kekagee, with a mixture of golden pippins, are most esteemed in this county [Cork] for making the best and strongest cider', adding in a footnote that 'the fruit is originally from Ireland, and the cider is much valued in that country'. Cider made from Cockagee apples could even pass for wine – according to Robert Hogg's account from 1851, 'The cyder is of the colour of sherry (or rather of French white wine), and every whit as fine and clear. ... It hath a more vinous taste than any cyder I ever drank, and as the sight might deceive a curious eye for wine, so I believe the taste might pass an incurious palate for the same liquor.'

Despite being one of the oldest and best cider apples, the Cockagee was believed to be extinct. The Irish Seed Savers Association thinks that it may have found it again, growing in an old orchard in Ennis, though research is still ongoing to determine if it is indeed the long-lost original.

In 2012, Armagh Bramley apples were given Protected Geographical Indication (PGI) status in recognition of their uniquely sharp, tart, clean taste compared to English Bramleys. Armagh's damp, mild climate is well suited for the production of cooking apples – Armagh orchards produce more than 40,000 tons of Bramley apples every year, many of which go towards making cider. Armagh Cider Co., who grow and use their own Bramley apples, are therefore entitled to use the PGI logo on their bottles of Carsons Crisp and Maddens Mellow.

How do you like them apples: Cider goes big

Cider hung on to its homespun roots for much longer than beer did – it was a farmhouse product until the late 1940s, when apple presses and crushing machines stopped travelling from farm to farm and farmers became more specialised. In the early decades of the twentieth century,

local authorities in south Tipperary and Waterford even employed an instructor to help farmers in the region to hone their cider-making skills, who then sold it to locals and publicans. As in other cider-producing regions, such as the UK and France, cider was even used to pay rent and farm workers' wages in certain parts of Ireland.

How did all this cider come to be made on farms in the first place? '[W]ith the emergence of the independent farming class in the late nineteenth and early twentieth centuries, a major expression of their newfound confidence was the planting of small orchards and soft fruit bushes, mirroring the culture of the Big House,' writes Regina Sexton in *A Little History of Irish Food*. 'This is still very much the case today, and many rural households will have a dozen apple trees and a cluster of blackcurrant and gooseberry bushes.' Several of Ireland's new artisan cider-makers, such as Daniel Emerson of Stonewell and Andrew Boyd of Kilmegan, were inspired to start making cider precisely because of such old farmhouse orchards on their family property.

In her book *Forgotten Skills of Cooking*, Darina Allen writes:

> Dick Keating … tells me that the practice of making cider on farms persisted in some places right up until the late 1940s. Originally, people would have gone to the distillery in Fethard and bought whiskey barrels which held 60–80 gallons to use to ferment their cider. What they didn't know was that the cider stripped the alcohol from the barrels, so the feisty brew that resulted ended up being about 20% proof. It earned the cider the nickname 'Johnny Jump-up'! Dick also remembers a travelling cider press mounted on horse and cart that went from farm to farm making cider right up to the 1940s. Local people could go along to the farm with a jug and get a flagon of cider for threepence.

The beginning of the end for farmhouse cider was in 1935, when William Magner bought an orchard, reopened the Murphy Brewery in Clonmel, Co. Tipperary, and started making cider on an industrial scale. In Ireland, Bulmers is to cider what Guinness is to beer – they dominated the market to such an extent that it was nearly impossible for others to compete, especially after British cider-maker H.P. Bulmer Ltd bought a 50% stake in 1937 and greatly increased production. Almost ten years later, in 1946, they took over the remaining 50% of the business and changed the name to Bulmers (although it is marketed as Magners everywhere else). H.P.

Bulmer Ltd, meanwhile, grew to become the largest cider-maker in the world – the seventeen brands under its belt account for more than half of the cider consumed in the UK. Today the company is part of the C&C Group, which has many other ciders in its portfolio, and Bulmers remains the best-selling cider in Ireland.

Just like beer, mass-produced cider is a multimillion-euro business in Ireland today. According to the Irish Cider Association, cider consumption has grown from less than 3% of the Irish market to more than 10% over the last twenty years, to the point that Irish people are now amongst the biggest consumers of cider in the world, at sixteen litres of cider per capita per year. A decade ago, in 2004, Ireland produced about 6% of the world's cider – not too shabby for a small island.

Artisan cider, on the other hand, accounts for a miniscule 0.08% of the Irish cider market. Of the 80–85 million litres of cider produced in Ireland each year, only 617,000 litres of that is craft cider – but that's up from 126,000 litres in 2012, a 489% increase, and this is expected to double yet again by 2016, to nearly 1.2 million litres. Small-scale cider production in the Republic hasn't benefited from the same duty rebates as craft beer, which is a sore point with cider-makers. Irish microbreweries are entitled to claim back 50% of the duty they pay, which has played a significant part in the current microbrewery boom. In Northern Ireland, however, no duty at all is charged if you make less than 7,000 litres of cider per year. All the same, it hasn't prevented the artisan cider industry from blossoming. Bord Bia, the Irish Food Board, notes that there is an increasing interest in Irish-produced and Irish-owned ciders here at home, so it would seem that there is plenty of scope for existing cider-makers to expand or for new ones to enter the market.

> Is deacair amhrán a rádh gan gloine. (It's hard to sing with an empty glass.)
> – Irish proverb

The cider revival

If craft beer is the poster boy of the Irish food and drink sector, then craft cider is its pretty, rosy-cheeked sister. In a similar way to craft beer, good-quality Irish cider is becoming far easier to find. While Ireland may have one of the highest levels of cider consumption in the world, until recently it was all about the big-brand, mass-produced, mass-marketed ciders. Now it's about Irish apples and people and places.

Despite Armagh's reputation as the Orchard County, there wasn't a single cider-maker there for half a century before Mac's Armagh Cider came onto the scene in 2000. Over a dozen new cider-makers have come on board in the past few years (see page 110). Many of these artisan cider-makers are going back to their farmhouse roots, using traditional production methods and apples from their own orchards (or failing that, 100% Irish apples) for a branch-to-bottle product.

Talking to the *Irish Examiner* in 2013, Daniel Emerson of Stonewell Irish Cider said that two factors have worked in craft cider's favour: 'One is the Magners effect, which has happened in the last ten to fifteen years – advertising by Bulmers/Magners has transformed the image of cider, making it fashionable and trendy again. The other factor is the growing popularity of craft beer, which is being used by publicans to offer a point of difference to attract customers during the recession. This has helped create an interest in other craft drinks.'

Craft cider is looking back to its classy past, when it was popular amongst the aristocracy and served in ornate flutes, and hopes to cultivate that kind of distinguished, refined association again. In fact, some of the best ciders have even been compared to champagne, and Belgian master sommelier Marc Stroobandt has observed that 'cider drinkers are now approaching cider with a sophistication similar to that of wine drinkers' – a comparison not lost on the cider producers, who are quick to tell you how well their product pairs with food. Emma Tyrrell of Cider Ireland says, 'We are seeing people serve a dry cider instead of champagne at wedding receptions. Maybe it's the "Buy Irish" thing, but served in a flute with canapés like black pudding bites and devils on horseback, it seems to go down a treat.'

It is clear that a little consumer education on craft cider is needed. The flip side of the 'Bulmers effect' is that we now expect cider to be very sweet, so your first experience of a dry, tannic cider can be quite startling. 'It's a bit of an uphill battle to persuade people that cider is a great (and low-alcohol) alternative to wine,' Emma continues. 'In the minds of most, cider is a teenage, behind-the-bike-shed drink. But the dry, vintage ciders that are available now are light years away from the confected cheap versions, and like wine, will vary slightly in taste from year to year.' One of the advantages of cider is that it can sway people from both the wine and beer camps, so its potential for food pairing needs to be appreciated too (see pages 140–141 for tips). So let's start by looking at what exactly cider is and how it's made, the different styles of cider and how to evaluate it.

JONAGO RED
CLASS 1
€ 7.50 PER BOX
6 KG (13.2 LBS)

What Is Cider?

Cider is a fermented alcoholic drink made from apples, produced by a cider-maker (or ciderist) in a cidery. That's basically it. The cider that we want to drink is made from Irish apples, not apple concentrate, and doesn't use artificial sweeteners such as glucose syrup, flavourings or colourings. The Irish Revenue definition of cider sets alcohol levels between 1.2% and 15% ABV. Other than that, unfortunately, there is no regulatory definition in Ireland of what constitutes a cider, much less a 'real', 'artisan' or 'craft' cider, which gives industrial producers the opportunity to put many other ingredients into the product besides apple juice – and they do.

> Sometimes our American friends muddy the waters by using the term 'apple cider' when what they are actually talking about is a dark, unfiltered, unpasteurised apple juice, not the alcoholic variety that we are used to, which they call 'hard cider'.

From Branch to Bottle: How to Make Cider

There are three main categories of apples: dessert or eating apples, cooking apples and cider apples. Production is evenly split between the three types of apples in Ireland, but Teagasc, the Irish Agriculture and Food Development Authority, has flagged the potential for more extensive cider apple production due to the increasing popularity of cider.

- **Dessert/eating apples:** Sweet and crisp, these can normally be eaten straight from the tree, e.g. Elstar, Jonagold, Katy, Worcester Pearmain.
- **Cooking/culinary apples:** Large and tart, these are used for cooking, e.g. Bramley.
- **Cider apples:** These have high sugar levels to promote fermentation and varying levels of acid and tannin, e.g. Ashton Bitter, Dabinett, Harry Jersey, Ten Commandments, Yarlington Mill.

Cider apples have more fibrous flesh than dessert or cooking apples, which makes it easier to squeeze out every last drop of juice. They are further subdivided into four categories, depending on acid and tannin levels. Ever had that dry, puckery feeling in your mouth after a sip of strong tea? That's the astringency from the tannins, which are also present in cider apples and well-made cider.

- **Sweets:** Low acid, low tannins. These are the blandest cider apple and are useful for blending with other varieties.
- **Sharps:** High acid, low tannins. These contribute an acid bite to cider.
- **Bittersweets:** Low acid, high tannins. These add bitterness to the cider.
- **Bittersharps:** High acid, high tannins. These balance out the blandness of sweets and the low acidity of bittersweets.

As with the type of grape used in wine, the variety of apple chosen will affect the final flavour of the cider. A skilled cider-maker blends a mixture of apples to achieve their ideal balanced and well-flavoured cider. A single variety of apple can also be used (and in fact, Irish cider-makers David Llewellyn and Toby's Handcrafted Cider have both made a single-varietal cider with Katy apples, while Stonewell Cider has made one with Elstar apples), but it can be difficult to produce a well-rounded cider this way – not that this stopped David Llewellyn from taking home a Pomme d'Or award at the 2014 International Cider Fair for his single-varietal Katy Reserve 2011 cider.

Like wine – and unlike beer – craft cider is a seasonal product. It is dependent on a harvest; it has a vintage and will vary a little in flavour from year to year; and as a result of the blending process, it will also vary from producer to producer. A true artisan cider has a lot of the character of its maker in it, as it is they who choose the nature and characteristics of the blend. Autumn, when the apples are ripe, is the busiest time of the year for artisan cider-makers. Big commercial cider-makers, on the other hand, make cider all year round from concentrate, or 'conc', which can be imported from anywhere in the world; our focus is on cider-makers who use freshly pressed juice from Irish apples.

The stages of making cider

1. **Selecting:** Good cider starts with good apple juice and the ciderist must carefully select the apples needed, often using several different varieties. Before they can be used, they must be washed, cleaned and sorted.

2. **Milling:** To get the juice from the apples, they first need to be shredded or milled into a pulp, called pomace.

3. **Pressing:** There are several different methods. The most traditional – and the most laborious, although efficient in terms of juice extraction – is called the rack and cloth press. It involves putting the milled apples into cloth-wrapped parcels, called cheeses, and stacking them on top of each other in the apple press. Press. Repeat. And again. More modern methods include pneumatic and belt presses.

4. **Fermenting:** The pure apple juice produced is transferred to a tank, pH and sugar levels are checked and a special yeast (often a wine or champagne yeast) can be introduced to initiate fermentation. Unlike the industrial producers, craft cider producers do not have jacketed tanks to heat up the juice and expedite the fermentation, but rather they depend on the ambient temperature. As such, this process can take one to two months.

5. **Maturing:** The cider is drawn (racked) off the lees, or spent yeast, and aged, preferably for a minimum of three months to round out the flavours, though it can be aged for anywhere up to two years.

6. **Blending:** The raw cider is tasted and blended with other raw ciders from different apple varieties or with apple juice, depending on what kind of cider is the designated end result. For example, Tempted? blends strawberry wine and apple juice with their base cider for their delectable strawberry cider at this stage.

7. **Carbonating:** While cider can be served still, most Irish ciders are carbonated in some way. This can be by bottle conditioning, by adding apple juice at bottling for a secondary fermentation (like Llewellyns Double L Bone Dry Cider) or by using carbon dioxide.

8. **Bottling and labelling:** Many of the small cider-makers still do this step by hand, making their ciders a truly handcrafted product from start to finish.

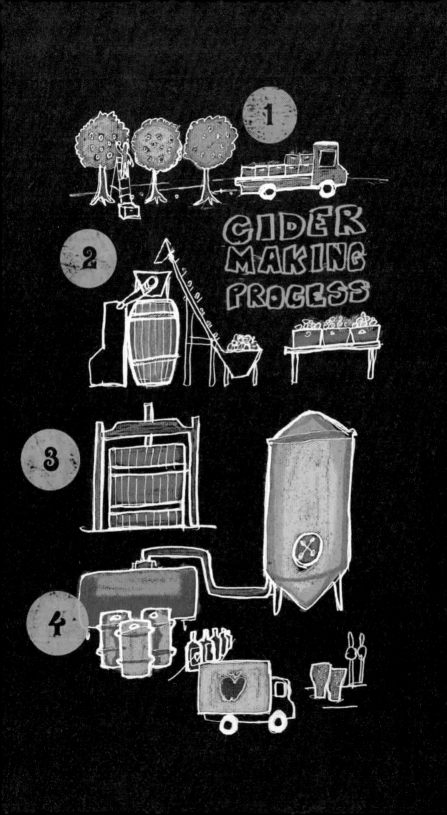

CIDER MAKING PROCESS

Cider Styles

- **Dry:** Clean and crisp with a refreshing acidity, which can be tongue-puckeringly tannic for the uninitiated.
- **Medium dry:** More body and a smoother mouthfeel than dry cider, with a little sweetness. These ciders go particularly well with food.
- **Sweet:** Full-bodied, with pronounced sweet apple flavours and a smooth finish.
- **Flavoured:** Also known as 'made wine'. Natural flavourings such as strawberry, elderflower and honey can be introduced at the blending stage.
- **Scrumpy:** A strong, tannic, cloudy cider style originally made in the West Country of England using traditional methods. Mac's 401 Belfast Scrumpy, made by Mac's Armagh Cider, is a traditional cider in this style.

Keeved cider is naturally sweet and sparkling with a deep colour, made by carefully controlling the fermentation. Keeving is a technique rather than a style and is popular in France, especially Brittany. Mark Jenkinson at The Cider Mill in Co. Meath currently makes Ireland's only keeved cider, called Cockagee Pure Irish Keeved Cider – well worth seeking out for real cider aficionados.

Making cider at home

Making cider isn't that difficult. In fact, if you've got a good crop on your apple tree at home, it's worth a try – after all, it's how a good few of Ireland's new artisan cider-makers got their start. Take some ripe apples, crush them into a coarse pulp, press to extract the juice and allow them to ferment. Of course, it's not quite that easy either, especially if you want to make something that's actually drinkable. A book like *Craft Cider Making* by Andrew Lea will set you on the right road. David Llewellyn also runs courses at Sonairte in Laytown, Co. Meath, in the autumn (see www.sonairte.ie for details).

Apple Cider

from *Forgotten Skills of Cooking* by Darina Allen (2009)

This is an old nineteenth-century recipe that is brilliantly easy to make, with no need to peel or press the apples.

Makes about 3 litres (just over 5 pints)

3kg (6½lb) cooking apples
900g (2lb) sugar
50g (2oz) fresh ginger
3 cinnamon sticks

Grate the apples into an enamel or stainless steel bucket and cover with 7½ litres (16 pints) of cold water. Stir with a sterilised wooden spoon every day for a week. Strain.

Stir the sugar into the juice. Then add the spices and leave to macerate for a day. Strain through clean muslin. Pour into sterilised bottles and seal well with screw-top lids.

Store in a cold dry place until Christmas.

How to Taste Cider

Just as you don't expect wine to taste like grapes or beer to taste like raw barley, there is more to cider than just apples. A cider can certainly taste appley, but it might only have the merest suggestion of apples. Cider can also have flavours and aromas of citrus fruit, wine or even the characteristic smoky bacon flavour of a dry English cider.

Evaluating cider is very similar to the way you approach beer, with the same factors coming into play – appearance, aroma, taste and texture – and a lot of the same descriptive vocabulary too. Appreciating these different elements will help you to better appreciate the complexity of cider, but at the end of the day it all comes down to your own personal preference and palate.

Appearance

Appearance can be broken down into three parts: carbonation, clarity and colour.

- **Carbonation:** Is the cider still or sparkling? This can range from completely flat to *pétillant* (moderate carbonation) to champagne-like levels of bubbles if the cider is highly carbonated.
- **Clarity:** Is the clarity brilliant, clear, slightly hazy, hazy or cloudy? Most cider-makers aim for a brilliantly clear cider, but there is nothing wrong with a slight haze in a more rustic, unfiltered farmhouse cider, such as those made by David Llewellyn.
- **Colour:** Cider can range in colour from pale straw to deep gold, even a pink reminiscent of rosé wine, all the way up to an apricot or amber hue, depending on what kind of apples were used.

Aroma

The aroma is a preview of the taste. It can be fruity, woody or yeasty, while traditional English ciders often have a farmyard note. Off aromas and flavours can include vinegar or solvents (acetic), butterscotch or toffee (diacetyl), chemicals, banana or tropical fruit (esters), leather, caramel, sherry or an overall sense of staleness (a sign of oxidation), or plastic, medicinal or smoky (phenolic) aromas and flavours.

Taste

The best ciders are balanced ciders. Cider's flavour ranges from dry to medium to sweet, but it should strike a happy medium between sweetness and a little brisk acidity to stimulate your palate.

- **Sweetness:** There are three levels of sweetness, which are based on the residual sugars (RS) in a finished cider: dry, medium and sweet. Dry ciders have less than 0.9% RS, medium ciders are between 0.9% and 4% RS, while sweet ciders are 4% and up. Bone-dry ciders will

have no residual sugar at all, while very sweet ciders can have as much as a dessert wine (10% RS and up).

- **Acidity:** A cider needs to have some acidity to balance out the sweetness and to make it clean and refreshing instead of cloying. However, it should never be so acidic as to make your mouth pucker.
- **Tannin:** A little tannin is needed to balance the cider. If the cider is too tannic, however, it can have an undesirable astringent, bitter quality that dries out your mouth.

Texture

This is the mouthfeel and body of a cider. Cider has a more subtle body than beer, while highly sparkling ciders will be similar to champagne. Many ciders have a mouthfeel like full-bodied white wine.

How to Serve Cider

We have Bulmers to thank for the notion that cider is best served in a pint glass packed full of ice. While this does make for a refreshing drink on a hot summer day, cold kills flavour and the melting ice will dilute it, so it is not the best way to appreciate a craft cider. Believe it or not, cellar temperature is good for cider, though lightly chilled (but not over ice!) is perfectly fine too. Putting a bottle of cider in the fridge half an hour before you want to drink it should do the trick.

At the height of cider's heyday, it was served in decorative flutes. Try serving your special craft cider in a champagne flute or pilsner glass to show off its sparkle and its pedigree.

Cider: A Drink for All Seasons

We have come to think of cider as an ice-cold summertime drink, but it is time to move beyond that and drink it all year round. 'True cider is often best served chilled, but not too chilled,' says Emma Tyrrell from Cider Ireland. 'Many artisan producers would suggest drinking it out of a stemmed wine glass, and certainly not over ice.' Or in the colder months of the autumn and winter, try mulling it with cinnamon, cloves, orange peel and a little sugar, just as we do with red wine during the holidays. The key here is to think of cider as an Irish alternative to imported white wine – our very own homegrown apple wine. And with producers like The Cider Mill and Stonewell Cider selling their ciders in 75cl bottles, why not set out a bottle for sharing at your next dinner party?

Apple Days

The first Apple Day in the UK was held in Covent Garden, London, in 1990. The festival was created by the Common Ground charity to celebrate apples, orchards and the rich variety and diversity of local foods that we shouldn't allow to be lost. It is now celebrated throughout the UK, including in Northern Ireland, and in some places it has become a weekend-long festival complete with games, demos, talks and of course apple juice and cider tastings.

In the Republic, the Organic Centre in Co. Leitrim hosts an annual Apple Day in October featuring guided orchard tours of their sixty apple trees, grafting and pruning demos and apple tress and seeds for sale, while Slow Food Ireland organised the first annual Apple and Craft Cider Festival in 2012 (see page 207 for more details).

CHAPTER 5

BLESSED ARE THE BREWERS AND CIDER-MAKERS

THE BREWERS

The Irish craft beer scene tends to fall into different generations, from the early birds like Hilden, who managed to survive solo since 1981 until they were joined in the late 1990s by some fellow pioneers, to the post-rebate gang between 2006 and 2011, an exciting crew who landed in 2013 and then the new wave of 2014.

First Generation: 1981 to Late 1990s

The first generation of the craft beer movement began in earnest in the mid 1990s in Ireland. Hilden Brewing, Porterhouse, Carlow Brewing, Whitewater Brewery and the Franciscan Well ploughed a lonely furrow back then, when craft beer was neither popular nor very profitable. But these were the early adopters, and the ones who stayed the course. Apart from Hilden, which was established in Northern Ireland in 1981, Ireland didn't have any microbreweries until the 1990s. The breweries that set up then included companies like Dublin Brewing Company in Smithfield, the Biddy Early brewpub in Co. Clare and Dwan's in Thurles, all now gone. These are the ones that stuck around:

Carlow Brewing Co.	Porterhouse
Franciscan Well	Whitewater
Hilden	

Brewery tours

If you'd like to visit a brewery, it is essential to contact them in advance rather than just turning up, or join a tour group such as Brewery Hops (see page 198), who arrange everything. Alternatively, keep an eye on individual breweries' social media and Beoir's website (www.beoir.org) for information on tasting events and festivals where you can meet the brewers and quiz them to your heart's content.

Carlow Brewing Company

Bagenalstown, Co. Carlow | www.carlowbrewing.com

Part of the first wave of Irish craft brewing, Seamus O'Hara set up the Carlow Brewing Company in 1996 and launched his first three beers in 1998. Like other breweries that were set up in the 1990s, they found it difficult to make headway against the big boys – there were 'lots of challenges along the way', says Seamus. But it didn't deter them. Rather than disappear, they thought laterally, knuckled down and started to produce Irish craft beer for the export market. With years of experience and several Brewing Industry International Awards under their belt, Carlow Brewing was well placed when Irish consumers started to demand more flavoursome beers. Formerly located next to the Carlow railway station, in 2009 the brewery outgrew its premises and moved down the road to Bagenalstown.

Seamus has worked hard to raise the profile of the industry and is the co-founder of the annual Irish Craft Beer and Cider Festival. 'We've found that any of the big events where people congregate usually have some big brewery sponsor that keeps us all out, so we said "let's do our own festival!" We're doing it together and it's working really well.' He strongly believes in co-operation between breweries: 'We're still a small part of the market, and working together helps to increase awareness. We all do our little bit to educate people about craft beer so we all win at the end of the day.'

Beers: Carlow Brewing produces its beers under the O'Hara's label: Amber Adventure, Curim Gold Celtic Wheat Beer, Double IPA, Irish Lager, Irish Pale Ale, Irish Stout, Leann Folláin, Traditional Red Ale

Franciscan Well Brewery and Brew Pub
Cork City | www.franciscanwellbrewery.com

In January 2013, big boys Molson Coors bought Cork's Franciscan Well beer brand and micro-brewery in a multimillion-euro deal, causing an almighty kerfuffle amongst craft beer devotees. Estimates at the time calculated that the speciality beer market would grow from the current €24 million to approximately €235 million of the total Irish beer market by 2017. Molson Coors was determined to get its own slice of that pie, and to that end announced that it had plans to expand the brewery's existing range of brands and set up a new 50hl brewery in Cork's Marina Commercial Park to boost the brewery's former capacity of 11.5hl – big changes for a tucked-away little brewpub that was set up in 1998 by Liam McNeill and Shane Long. The beer garden out the back plays host to some legendary festivals, most notably their annual cask ale and Easter beer fests.

Beer: Blarney Blonde, Chieftain IPA, Friar Weisse, Purgatory Pale Ale, Rebel Red, Shandon Stout

Hilden Brewery
Lisburn, Co. Antrim | www.hildenbrewing.com

Established in 1981 at a time of major political unrest in Northern Ireland, Hilden Brewery is Ireland's oldest independent brewery currently in operation. It was set up by Seamus and Ann Scullion (Ann was Ireland's first female brewer, or brewster) when they returned home after living in England and dis-covering the joys of real ale. While initially very successful, especially in the cask ale market (at the time, it was Northern Ireland's only microbrewery), the market dominance of large brewing companies meant some tough times during the late 1980s. But the couple didn't let grass grow under their feet. They set up a beer and music festival (see page 206) in 1984 and diversified into other related areas in the 1990s: the Tap Room Restaurant at Hilden and Molly's Yard restaurant in Belfast. Their son Owen, who understood that he would be doing a brewing degree at Edinburgh's Heriot-Watt University before he even knew what a degree was, joined the family business in 2005. He is now overseeing an expansion that will almost quadruple brewing capacity, from 4,000hl to 14,000hl, and Hilden's bottled beers are widely available throughout Ireland.

Beers: Barney's Brew, Belfast Blonde, Cathedral Quarter, Headless Dog, Hilden Ale, Hilden Halt, Hilden Irish Stout, Mill Street IPA, Nut Brown, Scullions Irish, Titanic Quarter, Twisted Hop

Porterhouse Brewing Company
Blanchardstown, Dublin 15 | www.porterhousebrewco.com

Many Dubliners got their first taste of craft beer from taps at the Porterhouse Temple Bar, Ireland's first brewpub, which opened in 1996. Finding decent beer amidst the hen and stag party madness was a surprise; the fact that it was Irish had us hooked. Founders Liam LaHart and Oliver Hughes had already been through a couple of failed breweries – Dempsey's of Inchicore and Harty's of Blessington both opened and closed in the early 1980s – but they put their experience to good use in Porterhouse, where the microbrewery was the centrepiece of the bar. Head brewer Peter Mosley came on board not long after they opened in Temple Bar and he now runs the brewery at a separate site in Blanchardstown, with a 65hl traditional infusion mash brewhouse. As the Porterhouse group grew and demand for their products increased – they now have three bars in Dublin and one in Bray, and have also expanded to Cork, London and New York – Dublin city centre brewing ceased in 2002. Porterhouse is considered to be one of the early pioneers of the craft beer scene in Ireland and their beers are top notch.

Beers: Porterhouse brews the widest range of any Irish microbrewery, with a good selection of regulars that are available in bottles and on draught from the Porterhouse pubs: Brainblásta, Celebration Stout, Chiller, Hersbrucker, Hop Head, Oyster Stout, Plain, Red, Temple Bräu, TSB, Wrasslers XXXX

Whitewater Brewery
Kilkeel, Co. Down | www.whitewaterbrewery.com

'How do you make a small fortune in the brewing industry?' asks Whitewater owner Bernard Sloan. 'Start with a big fortune!' After having survived in the industry since 1996, Bernard has seen plenty of breweries come and go. Looking around him at the 2013 Irish Craft Beer and Cider Festival, he couldn't resist cautioning that 'there's no easy money to be made'. It might not be easy money, but Whitewater is now Northern Ireland's largest microbrewery and its products are widely stocked in supermarkets throughout Ireland. It also owns the CAMRA award-winning White Horse Inn at Saintfield, Co. Down, which boasts a large range of Whitewater beers on cask and keg, along with a menu that features locally sourced food. It's worth searching out their Clotworthy Dobbin, a rich ruby ale that was named as one of the World's Fifty Best Beers in 2007 by judges in the International Beer Challenge.

Beers: Bee's Endeavour, Belfast Ale, Belfast Black, Belfast Lager, Clotworthy Dobbin, Copperhead Pale Ale, Hoppelhammer

Brewhouse sizes

When you're talking to a brewer about their set-up, they'll inevitably mention the size of their brewhouse – but their terms of measurement can range from litres (l) to hectolitres (1hl = 100 litres) and even barrels or kegs. To avoid confusion, we are sticking to hl to give you a comparative idea of brewery sizes, which range from Beoir Chorca Dhuibhne, with a 4hl brewhouse, right up to Carlow Brewing Company's 65hl brewery.

Second Generation: Mid 2000s to 2011

After the pioneers came the establishers. A lot of the people behind these breweries had travelled widely, supped beers in all four corners of the globe and wondered why the hell Ireland didn't have a decent pint on offer. When the tax rebate for microbreweries was signed into being by Brian Cowan, the then Finance Minister, in 2005, it ushered in a new era, benefiting the first generation of breweries that had hung on by the skin of their teeth for years, and bringing a new gang on board, starting with Galway Hooker Brewery. Also part of this generation was the Ards Brewing Company, who began brewing and releasing limited amounts in 2011. Owner Charles Ballantyne is working on expanding the brewery in 2014.

Ards Brewing Co.	Elbow Lane*
Beoir Chorca Dhuibhne	Galway Bay
(West Kerry Brewery)	Galway Hooker
Bo Bristle	Inishmacsaint
Brown Paper Bag Project*	Kinnegar
Burren Brewery	Metalman
Carrig Brewing Co.	The 5 Lamps
Clanconnel Brewing Co.*	Trouble Brewing
Dingle Brewing Co.	White Gypsy
Donegal Brewing Co.	
Dungarvan Brewing Co.	
Eight Degrees	*Beer brewed by contract

Beoir Chorca Dhuibhne (West Kerry Brewery)

Ballyferriter, Co. Kerry | www.westkerrybrewery.ie

If you've ever driven the Slea Head Drive on the Dingle Peninsula, you've passed by Beoir Chorca Dhuibhne, known amongst non-gaelgoirs as the West Kerry Brewery. You may have been too gobsmacked by the views to notice, or, looking for shelter, you might have stopped off in Tig Bhric for lunch and succumbed to a pint from the afore-mentioned brewery. Beoir Chorca Dhuibhne started brewing in 2008 after being set up by the proprietors of Tig Bhric (Bricks) and the nearby Tigh Uí Chatháin (Kanes) – Adrienne Heslin, Paul O Loingsigh and Donal O Cathain – to provide local beer to their customers. Now run by Adrienne and Paul, Beoir Chorca Dhuibhne is one of Ireland's smallest microbreweries, brewing just 400 litres at a time. But word is spreading beyond Dingle. Their cask-conditioned beers are often available at festivals, and the bottle-conditioned Béal Bán (golden ale, with added rosehips), Cúl Dorcha (a dark, fruity red ale) and Carraig Dubh (a smooth, traditional porter) can also be tracked down at independent off-licences. Tours are available by appointment, but if the door is open they also welcome passers-by.

Beers: Béal Bán, Carraig Dubh, Cúl Dorcha

Bo Bristle

Banagher, Co. Offaly | www.bobristle.com

Bo Bristle was set up in 2010 when Englishman Andy Horn moved to Co. Offaly and teamed up with local man Morgan Smyth. We spotted them at the short-lived Brewers on the Bay beer festival in 2011 under their original name, Breweyed. They didn't officially launch as Bo Bristle until the Irish Craft Beer and Cider Festival in 2012. The brewery is based in the 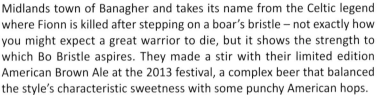 Midlands town of Banagher and takes its name from the Celtic legend where Fionn is killed after stepping on a boar's bristle – not exactly how you might expect a great warrior to die, but it shows the strength to which Bo Bristle aspires. They made a stir with their limited edition American Brown Ale at the 2013 festival, a complex beer that balanced the style's characteristic sweetness with some punchy American hops.

Beers: Amber Ale, IPA, Pilsner Lager, Red Ale

Brown Paper Bag Project

www.brownpaperbagproject.com

There are brewers who start their business by doing contract brewing with another microbrewery, and then there are nomadic or gypsy brewers like the Brown Paper Bag Project. The people behind it are the L. Mulligan Grocers trio of Colin Hession, Seáneen Sullivan and Michael Fogarty along with 'brewer extraordinaire' Brian Short. They collaborate with existing breweries, using their equipment to create special one-off beers – and then they move on. Launched in late 2012 with Dr Rudi, a strong  (7.4%) single-hop Belgian-style ale that was brewed at Eight Degrees, they have since developed an impressively diverse portfolio, brewed all over Europe, that refuses to accept limitations and has included the smooth, chocolatey Oxman brown ale, a champagne-finished Belgian tripel and Gøse, which incorporates sea salt and coriander in a soured mash. With no plans to settle down just yet – 'We're having heaps of fun travelling around meeting interesting people, discovering new styles and making beer in creative ways,' says Colin – it's worth keeping an eye on Twitter (@BrownPaperBagP) to see their next move.

Beers: Take a stroll into L. Mulligan Grocers and ask what's on offer!

Burren Brewery

Lisdoonvarna, Co. Clare | www.roadsidetavern.ie

'Oh, Lisdoonvarna/Lisdoon, Lisdoon, Lisdoon, Lisdoonvarna!' Christy Moore's paean to the Clare town in the mid 1980s didn't exactly concentrate on craft beer, focusing more on 'bottles – barrels – flagons – cans ... And they drinkin' pints to bate the band'. It's a long, long way from there to here, and now Roadside Tavern proprietor Peter Curtin, never afraid of a new venture, has a 2.5hl microbrewery based in his pub. It came about as a direct result of Peter's friendship with Gerry Dobbin, brother of master brewer Brendan Dobbin, who was also involved in setting up the Porterhouse. Brendan fabricated the equipment especially for Burren Brewery, and it now produces a lager (Burren Gold), a red ale (Burren Red) and a stout (Burren Black), which you can sup in what the *McKennas' Guides* calls 'one of County Clare's finest pubs'. You won't want to hurry away, as the bar also offers good pub grub, particularly smoked fish (which goes well with Burren Black, says Peter) from another family venture, the Burren Smokehouse, alongside Burren Black Stout ice cream and Burren Red bread.

Beers: Burren Black, Burren Gold, Burren Red

Carrig Brewing Company
Drumshanbo, Co. Leitrim | www.carrigbrewing.com

Remember Bo Peep jams? They were made in Drumshanbo by Lairds, in a factory that was once one of the largest in Europe. Closed in 1998, the space has since become a food hub and is now home to Sinead O'Connell and Martie Deegan's Carrig Brewing Company. The first brewery in Leitrim in 150 years, they started off by having their Carrig Lager and Rower's Red brewed under contract at Bo Bristle, launching the beers in 2012. Now, with their own brewhouse installed and doctor-of-philosophy-turned-brewer Andrew Jorgensen in situ, they have been developing an exciting variety of beers. They also want to acknowledge the history of the hub – and the fact that Sinead's grandmother supplied fruit to the factory in the 1940s and 1950s – by working on some fruit-orientated seasonal brews.

Beers: Brazen Amber Ale, Carrig Summer Pils, Carrig Lager Pipers Pale Ale, Poachers Pale Ale, Rower's Red

Clanconnel Brewing Company
Craigavon, Co. Armagh | www.clanconnelbrewing.com

Mark Pearson picked up the craft beer bug when he was working in Copenhagen, doing some committed research at brewpub Bryggeriet Apollo. With courses in how to set up a microbrewery at the University of Sunderland and a brewing course at York under his belt, he set up Clanconnel in Waringstown, Co. Down, in 2008. Clanconnel has a 1hl pilot brew plant that is used for R&D and the range of six beers is currently brewed by Hilden. The beer is branded under the McGrath's name – Master McGrath being a famous greyhound in the 1800s – with each style numbered and colour coded.

Beers: All sold under the McGrath's label: Irish Red Ale #1, Irish Pale Ale #2, Irish White Ale #3, Irish Black Stout #4, Irish Blonde Ale #5, Irish Amber Ale #6

Dingle Brewing Company

Dingle, Co. Kerry | www.dinglebrewingcompany.com

A former Kerry Group creamery turned micro-brewery is the home of the Dingle Brewing Company, which was set up by local businessman Jerry O'Sullivan in 2011. The focus is on making one beer: Tom Crean's Lager, a light, golden lager named after the legendary explorer from Annas-caul, Co. Kerry. While the lager hasn't travelled quite as far as its namesake (who completed three Antarctic expeditions before retiring home to run the South Pole Inn until his death in 1938), it is flying high, as it is now available in cans on Aer Lingus flights.

Beer: Tom Crean's Lager

Donegal Brewing Company

Ballyshannon, Co. Donegal | www.donegalbrewingcompany.com

Brendan O'Reilly is a far-sighted man. Owner of Dicey Reilly's Bar and Off-Licence in Ballyshannon, which has been run by his family for the last thirty-nine years, he headed to Sunderland University in 1997 to do his first brewing course, following that with a week-long course in the Porterhouse. But it wasn't the right time to bring craft beer to the homeplace of Rory Gallagher and he waited until Christmas 2012 to finally get his purpose-built 10hl brewery off the ground. His mainstay is Donegal Blonde, an easy-drinking golden ale that he describes as 'a good stepping stone into craft beers'. As well as making beer, he also stocks 500 world beers in the off-licence and has five rotation taps in the bar: 'We are continually bringing in different kegs, mainly Irish, so we can see at first hand what is trending at the moment.' Brendan has also been known to test out new brews on pub customers, so if you're stopping off along the Wild Atlantic Way, you might just need to book a room in Ballyshannon for the night.

Beers: Donegal Blonde and occasional specials

Dungarvan Brewing Company

Dungarvan, Co. Waterford | www.dungarvanbrewingcompany.com

It's a family affair at Dungarvan Brewing. Head brewer Cormac O'Dwyer, along with his wife Jen Uí Dhuibhir, his sister Claire Dalton and her husband Tom, launched the brewery in April 2010. Cormac has always loved traditional cask- and bottle-conditioned beer, which Dungarvan has become noted for. For the uninitiated who wants to know how their cask beer is dispensed, Claire asks them to think of the pub in *Coronation Street*. Even if you aren't a fan of the soap, you probably remember the handpump in the Rovers Return, behind which a variety of barmaids alternately glowered and simmered and stomped around in leopard print. The brewery has a solid rotation of seasonal specials, including a smooth, full-flavoured Coffee and Oatmeal Stout for wintertime, which uses oats from Flahavan's Mills in Kilmacthomas and Badger & Dodo coffee from Fermoy.

Beers: Black Rock Irish Stout, Copper Coast Red Ale, Helvick Gold Blonde Ale. Seasonals: Mahon Falls Rye Pale Ale (spring), Comeragh Challenger Irish Bitter (summer), Coffee and Oatmeal Stout (winter).

Eight Degrees Brewing
Mitchelstown, Co. Cork | www.eightdegrees.ie

Darina Allen described them as two cocky foreign guys; Caroline has been known to call them worse. When Kiwi Scott Baigent and Aussie Cameron Wallace set up EDB in 2011, it was with the aim of producing the kind of beers that they loved to drink back in their respective homelands. Drawn to and rooted in Ireland by two Irish women – Caroline is married to Scott, while Pamela took on Cam – they decided to set up their brewery in Mitchelstown, at the foot of the Galtee Mountains. A Kiwi and an Aussie going into business together? Anything for a good pint, and the lads, with the calming assistance of head brewer Mike Magee, have been producing plenty of those. They started 2014 in style when their one-festival-only beer, Amber-Ella, took a bronze medal at the brewers' equivalent of the Olympics, the World Beer Cup. It was a particularly cheeky win, given that they entered an American-style beer into an American awards process and beat the Americans at their own game.

Beers: Amber-Ella, Barefoot Bohemian Pilsner, Howling Gale Ale, Knockmealdown Porter, Sunburnt Irish Red and regular limited editions

Elbow Lane
Cork City | www.elbowlane.ie

The recipes for Cork's Elbow Lane beers were formulated with food in mind, says owner Conrad Howard. That's not surprising, as Elbow Lane – a brewery and a restaurant – brings to four the number of restaurants Conrad is involved in. The beer R&D was done back in 2012 at UCC's pilot brewery (we bet there were plenty of students willing to work on that project), and it was initially contract brewed at White Gypsy. The next logical step is to install their own brewhouse. The plan is that you'll be able to see the brewery at work while you eat – guaranteed to build up a thirst for the beers, which are only available in Elbow Lane and fellow restaurants Market Lane, The Castle and Orzo.

Beers: Angel Stout, Elbow Lager, Wisdom Ale

Galway Bay Brewery
Salthill, Co. Galway | www.galwaybaybrewery.com

The Galway Bay Brewery has become a bona fide
Irish craft beer juggernaut. Galway locals Jason
O'Connell and Niall Walsh owned a few pubs in
the city before opening a microbrewery at their
Oslo bar in Salthill in 2009. They didn't stop there.
They headed across the country to Dublin to
expand their mini-empire, and they now run five
bars in the capital (Against the Grain, Alfie Byrnes,
The Black Sheep, The Brew Dock and The Dark Horse) in addition to their
quartet in Galway (The Cottage Bar, The Oslo, The Salthouse Bar, The
Scholar's Rest). As Porterhouse has proven, if you already own a brewery,
it makes good financial sense to have some tied houses, and all the bars
have an extensive selection of GBB beers on tap alongside a range of Irish
and international craft brews. Head brewer Chris Treanor is sticking with
sea-themed names for the beers he produces, which include the dry and
dark Stormy Port porter and a lusciously hopped double IPA called Of
Foam and Fury that created quite a stir on its November 2013 release and
was justifiably voted as Beoir's beer of the year.

Beers: Bay Ale, Buried at Sea, Full Sail, Of Foam and Fury, Stormy Port

Galway Hooker Brewery
Oranmore, Co. Galway | www.galwayhooker.ie

The first of the second wave of microbreweries,
Galway Hooker Brewery was set up in 2006 by
cousins Aidan Murphy and Ronan Brennan. After
spending time in the US, Germany and the UK and
enjoying the range of beers that were on offer there,
not to mention observing the establishment of
Porterhouse and Carlow Brewing, Aidan believed that
there was a gap in the Irish market for something
different. He did his research by working in places like Okells Brewery in
the Isle of Man and completing a masters in brewing and distilling at Heriot-
Watt in Edinburgh before they launched their flagship, Galway Hooker, in
2006. Named after the iconic Galway Bay boat, it was in eight pubs that
summer, but proved to be a hard sell at the start. People were unwilling to
taste it or were aghast at the flavour: 'It looks like Heineken, but it doesn't
taste like Heineken!' Irish beer drinkers have come a long way since then.

Beers: Galway Hooker Irish Pale Ale, Galway Hooker Stout

Inishmacsaint Brewing Company
Derrygonnelly, Co. Fermanagh

Gordon Fallis doesn't do things in the most straight-forward way. Established in 2009, his Inishmacsaint Brewing Company has a brewkit installed in an old milking parlour and he occasionally uses a cave on his farm to cold-condition some of his experimental beers. Inspired by the rustic farmhouse ales of Belgium and northern France, Gordon uses local ingredients like bog myrtle, meadowsweet and spruce tips in his beer, and as part of his efforts to maintain the brewery as a sustainable farm project, he even grows hops, including Fuggle, Northern Brewer and East Kent Golding. His beers are unfiltered, unpasteurised and bottle conditioned – or cave conditioned – on site.

Beers: Fermanagh Beer, Lough Erne Brown Porter

Kinnegar Brewing Company
Rathmullan, Co. Donegal | www.kinnegarbrewing.ie

Trading up from being a nano to a microbrewery in 2013 kept Kinnegar Brewing Company owners Rick LeVert and Libby Carton busy, but it has paid off. Available locally in Donegal outlets like Rathmullan House since 2011, by the end of 2013 it was becoming easier to track down their beers as far south as Bradley's Off-Licence in Cork. While the self-proclaimed 'Small brewery. Big Beers' was no longer so small, going from a brewing capacity of only 120 litres a week to a 10hl brewhouse, the beers are still big, bold and experimental. A perfect example is Devil's Backbone Amber Ale, an unfiltered beer that pours a rich copper colour and has flavours of burnt toffee and dried fruit, perfect with the sweetness of roast pork.

Beers: Devil's Backbone Amber Ale, Limeburner Pale Ale, Rustbucket Rye Ale, Scraggy Bay IPA, Yannaroddy Coconut Porter

Metalman Brewing Company
Tycor, Co. Waterford | www.metalmanbrewing.com

Gráinne Walsh used to be a manager at Amazon.com, doing a bit of home brewing with her partner Tim Barber. In 2011 she decided to become one of Ireland's few brewsters, or female brewers, when she and Tim set up Metalman, named after a landmark on the Waterford coast. She

didn't leave her old life totally behind, though. Their flagship Metalman Pale Ale, a crisp session beer packed with vibrant citrus flavours, was inspired by her trips to Seattle with Amazon and what she calls 'the lovely West Coast hops that were being used in pale ales of that area at the time'. The beer was initially contract brewed by White Gypsy while Gráinne and Tim built up a customer base and set up their own brewery, which they got off the ground in 2012. Since then they have been brewing up a storm, and although their beers are currently only available on draught, Metalman may become one of the few Irish craft beers available in cans. Watch out at festivals for their ever-changing Chameleon, a playful range of experimental brews that has encompassed a lager, a rauchbier and a wheat beer. Gráinne is also actively involved in raising the profile of women in the brewing industry. For International Women's Day 2014, she co-ordinated Irish participation in an international collaborative brew day for female brewers when she, Adrienne Heslin from Beoir Chorca Dhuibhne and N17's Sarah Roarty got together to brew Unite Pale Ale.

Beers: Metalman Pale Ale. Seasonals: Alternator, Chameleon, Moonbeam, Windjammer.

The 5 Lamps Dublin Brewery
Dublin 8 | www.the5lampsbrewery.com

Set up in 2012 by Brian Fagan and part-owned by C&C Group, this brewery is based in Dublin's Liberties, in the shade of the slightly more famous (and considerably larger) Guinness at St James's Gate. Head brewer William Harvey had a twenty-six-year career with that behemoth before retiring and being subsequently persuaded to move into the microbrewery world. 'He does all the cool brewing stuff,' says Brian, 'while I do all the crap around it – bottling, admin, accounts!' Wanting to offer a Dublin alternative to the big brands, the 5 Lamps beers have local

associations, taking in locations like Blackpitts and the Liberties, even commemorating murdered woman Honor Bright, who lived around the corner from the brewery until her death in 1925.

Beers: 5 Lamps Dublin Lager, Blackpitts Porter, Honor Bright Red Ale, Liberties Dublin Ale

Trouble Brewing
Kill, Co. Kildare | www.troublebrewing.ie

With their distinctive pop art labels, it's easy to spot Trouble Brewing, which is run by cousins Paul O'Connor and Stephen Clinch. According to Paul, 'The idea behind the whole enterprise is to have a beer that's fun, that's enjoyable, a little bit irreverent and forward-thinking as well.'

Their first beer was brewed on St Patrick's Day 2010 – an auspicious day to start an Irish microbrewery. One of our favourite brews is their Dark Arts Porter, which started off initially as a limited edition, but it wasn't long before Paul and Stephen knew that it was a keeper. A dark, rich and malty brew with complex notes of coffee and dark chocolate, it is an end-of-meal tipple, something to savour with a chocolate brownie (like the ones on page 186, perhaps?) or a revelation when paired with a creamy tiramisu.

Beers: Dark Arts Porter, Deception Golden Ale, Sabotage IPA and an increasing number of limited edition specials

White Gypsy

Templemore, Co. Tipperary | www.whitegypsy.ie

The fingerprints of Cuilán Loughnane are all over the Irish brewing scene. After first encountering good beer in Canada and doing some brewing there, he came back to Ireland and worked at Dwan's Brewery in Thurles from 1997. Within a couple of years he was running that brewery and exporting a variety of cask beers to the UK. By 2002, the market had disappeared and Cuilán subsequently became head brewer at Messrs Maguire in Dublin, working on the in-house brewkit to make their beers and using surplus capacity to develop his own recipes. In 2009, he set up his White Gypsy brewery in his hometown of Templemore. As a contract brewer he has had a hand in helping other breweries to get started, including Metalman and Elbow Lane. He strongly believes in developing a sustainable brewing industry from the farmers up. To that end, he grows his own hops – 500 plants of a new dwarf variety, aroma hop First Gold, went in next to the brewery in spring 2014 – and uses Irish barley, with Emerald being his flagship all-Irish beer. Taking cues from the wine industry, Cuilán produces 75cl bottles of speciality beers, brewed to accompany food. The German doppelbock from that range has delicious flavours of toffee and fruit that make it especially good with venison, a Mexican mole sauce or even a smooth crème brûlée.

Beers: Amber Pale Ale, American Pale Ale, Belgian Dubbel, Blond Weiss (draught only), German Doppelbock, Russian Imperial Stout, Ruby Red Ale

Third Generation: 2013

While things went a little quiet during 2012, there was a lot of planning going on behind the scenes and the third generation of microbreweries hit the ground running in 2013, when it seemed like you couldn't go more than a few weeks without encountering another news story about the runaway success of Irish craft beer in the news.

There was also a certain amount of contract brewing, with some start-ups brewing their beer in another brewery before they invested in their own brewkit. Is this a problem? Not necessarily – many of the people who started off with contract-brewed beer in the second generation have since gone on to brew their own. The problem is when a brewery tries to pass off UK-brewed beer as Irish. No one likes being taken for a fool, and craft beer drinkers can be particularly vocal about it.

Blacks of Kinsale	Rye River
Brú Brewery	Sheelin
J.W. Sweetman	Stone Barrel*
Mountain Man*	West Mayo Brewery
Otterbank*	
Rascal's Brewing	*Beer brewed by contract*

Contract brewing

Building your own microbrewery doesn't come cheap. It involves begging (in the form of grant aid) and borrowing from any bank crazy enough to lend money. We try to draw the line at stealing. But what do you do if you have a recipe and a brand ready to go but are still waiting on your brewkit? For many start-ups, contract brewing (paying to use another brewery's equipment) has been a way to launch their first beers into the world and get their names out there before they can invest in the infrastructure needed to brew their own. But the line between entrepreneurship and speculation can be a fine one, and especially after the sale of the Franciscan Well to Molson Coors in 2013, there are some people out there who are more interested in jumping on the craft beer bandwagon than actually brewing beer. But there's more to being a brewery than just coming up with your own labels to slap on contract-brewed bottles. We have included all the breweries and contract brewers (denoted with an asterisk in the lists on pages 91, 104 and 109) that are currently producing beer in Ireland. For an up-to-the minute list of who's who and what's what, scroll through Beoir's A to Z list of Ireland's beer and cider at www.beoir.org.

Blacks of Kinsale

Kinsale, Co. Cork | www.kinsalecraftbrewery.com

Cork's gourmet capital has been associated with craft beer since Kinsale Brewing Company opened in 2001. KBC closed in the mid 2000s but now there's a new brewery in town, founded by Sam and Maudeline Black. The brewery was crowdfunded, giving 'the public the chance to be involved in the craft beer revolution', as Sam says. It wasn't just the Irish public that was interested; funding came from all over the world, including the US, the Netherlands and the UK, raising almost €2k over their €5k target. One large chunk came courtesy of Beoir members. Forty of them clubbed together so that they could spend a day doing a brew with Sam, taking home bottles of beer, the experience of brewing on a large scale and a real sense of engagement with the brand.

Beers: Black IPA, Hop Magnet Double IPA, Kinsale Pale Ale, Session Pale Ale

Brú Brewery

Trim, Co. Meath | www.brubrewery.ie

Dáire Harlin and Paddy Hurley were busy in 2013. The brewery, a medium-sized 17.5hl plant, was installed in July, and by September they were setting out their stall at the Irish Craft Beer and Cider Festival. Former solicitor Dáire initially came up with the idea of setting up a distillery before discovering that they couldn't afford it – but they could get funding for a brewery. Believing that there is a niche in the market to produce drinkable beers – 'not too hoppy, not too crazy' – Dáire plans to establish Brú in this area before brewing the 'mad stuff' that he would really like to make.

Beers: Brú Dubh Nitro Stout, Brú Lager, Brú Rí IPA, Brú Rua. Specials: Brú Bán, Brú Beo, Brú Mór.

J.W. Sweetman
Dublin 2 | www.jwsweetman.ie

This brewpub, first set up in 1998, was originally named Messrs Maguire, but by 2013 it had come under new management and was rebranded as J.W. Sweetman. As Messrs Maguire it had some distinctive brewers – Cuilán Loughnane was there before setting up White Gypsy and Melissa Camire, from Washington, DC, briefly brought a refreshing US influence to the Irish craft beer scene from 2010 to 2011. With an enviable location overlooking O'Connell Bridge, it is now Dublin's only brewpub, with head brewer Rob Hopkins – who is also a gypsy brewer, trading under the name Barrelhead – running the on-site brewery. J.W. Sweetman serve their own beers on tap (and do a neat tasting tray of the core range), along with a wide selection of other Irish and international craft beers, while their comprehensive food menu focuses on matching beer and food. They also sell and fill their own growlers.

Beers: Irish Red Ale, Kölsch, Pale Ale, Porter, Weiss, regular seasonals

Mountain Man Brewing
Renanirree, Co. Cork | www.mountainmanbrewing.com

Once a mountain man, always a mountain man, and Phil Cullen won't forget his Knocknarea mountain roots even though he's now based in the Derrynasaggarts in West Cork. A former home brewer, he met Gordon Lucey, head brewer at the 9 White Deer Brewery in Ballyvourney, on a brewery course in 2012 and they decided to collaborate, combining Phil's know-how with Gordon's brewing equipment. While 9 White Deer was being built, Phil  contract brewed his first two beers in 2013: Green Bullet, using the eponymous New Zealand hops, and the coppery English-style IPA Hairy Goat. His first brew at 9 White Deer was summer 2014's Crazy Horse San Diego IPA. Tongue-in-cheek branding has made Mountain Man stand out from the pack – and he's got the beers to support him.

Beers: Crazy Horse San Diego IPA, Green Bullet, Hairy Goat

Sheelin Brewery

Enniskillen, Co. Fermanagh | www.sheelin.com

Irish brewers have a rich backstory, coming to the beer world from many different lines of work, but George Cathcart is the first pharmacist with a PhD in biomolecular sciences that we have come across. He brings his expertise in enzymology and microbiology – the two key sciences in the brewing process – to the table, along with a passion for food, to create a high-quality local product. It's no wonder his Sheelin Blonde Ale has been going down so well since its launch in April 2013.

Beer: Sheelin Blonde Ale

West Mayo Brewery

Islandeady, Co. Mayo | www.westmayobrewery.com

The first microbrewery in Mayo – but not the last – Iain and Caroline Price launched West Mayo Brewery in July 2013 with a draught red ale offering called Clew Bay Sunset. The five-barrel brewery is based on their farm, with the brewing leftovers going directly to their cattle. 'They love the spent grains,' comments Iain, although the more bitter ingredients are not favourites. 'They also eat the hops, but less quickly!' Growing on the farm is bog myrtle, a traditional pre-hop beer adjunct, which Iain uses, along with Pilgrim hops, to flavour their Paddy's Pilgrims Porter. With the aim of offering local beer on draught, their focus is on producing kegs, which are now stocked in bars throughout the county.

Beers: Clew Bay Sunset, Clifford's Connacht Champion, Paddy's Pilgrims Porter

A few new players launched beers towards the end of 2013, including Dublin's Stone Barrel Brewing and gypsy brewer Otterbank Brewing. Rye River Brewing released their heavily branded McGargle's range, while Rascal's Brewing launched with a ginger porter that they had made at Brú Brewery, the result of winning the 2013 National Homebrew Club competition. Both Rye River and Rascal's went on to launch their own breweries in 2014.

Fourth Generation: 2014

You thought there were a lot of start-ups in 2013? Wait until you see what happened during 2014! While Ireland may not yet be at the US rate of 1.2 breweries opening every day (well, they do have the advantage of having 8% of the overall beer market), we're working hard to catch up. The Irish craft beer market needs to expand its market share to more than 1%, and fast. We don't want to end up with more producers than consumers! The good news, though, is that every one of these breweries plays its own part in spreading the word about craft beer. Families and friends get press-ganged into helping out, are offered a taste, and before you know it they're talking with real knowledge about beer styles and hops. Places like Cork's Cotton Ball, a traditional Mayfield pub that has been in the Lynch family since 1874, are now brewing their own, giving their customers a real, tangible introduction to the idea of something outside the mainstream.

These start-ups are also looking beyond the holy trinity of pale ale/red ale/stout. At Westport's Mescan Brewery, veterinarians-turned-brewers Killian Ó Mórín and Bart Adons take Bart's homeplace as their inspiration for their Belgian-style beers. Just down the road in Tuam, Sarah Roarty launched her N17 Brewery with a smooth, complex rye ale. The West is awake, and brewing.

9 White Deer, Cork
Black Donkey, Roscommon
Blackstairs, Wexford*
Brehon Brewhouse,
    Monaghan
Clearsky, Tyrone*
Cloughmore, Down*
Cotton Ball, Cork
Farmageddon Brewing
    Co-op, Down
Four Provinces, Dublin*
Hercules, Antrim
Hillstown Brewery, Antrim
Independent Brewing Co.
    of Ireland, Galway

Jack Doyle's, Wexford
Little Island, Cork*
Mescan Brewery, Mayo
Muckish Mountain,
    Donegal*
Munster Brewery, Cork
N17 Brewery, Galway
Pokertree, Tyrone
Red Hand, Tyrone
Rising Sons, Cork*
St Mel's, Longford
White Hag, Sligo

Beer brewed by contract

THE CIDER-MAKERS

Despite Ireland's long history of orchards and apple production, the production of artisan cider has only really taken off in the past few years. Until the recent craft cider revival, Northern Ireland was the only apple-growing area in the UK that didn't have its own cider producers. That has all changed now. Mac's Armagh Cider, the grandfather of the Armagh 'revivalist' cider movement, led the way when they planted their cider apple orchards in 1995 and started producing cider in 2000, while David Llewellyn became the first producer to sell cider in the south. The past five years have seen a small burst of activity, to the point that there are now seventeen craft cider producers on the island of Ireland.

Even though there are only a few producers, they are making a surprisingly varied range of ciders, from Highbank Orchard's honeyed organic Medieval Cider to Kilmegan's cider infused with wild elderflowers and Tempted?'s cider made with strawberry wine, and everything dry, sweet and sparkling in between.

Armagh Cider Company*
Cider Mill*
Craigies Irish Cider*
Dan Kelly's Cider*
Dovehill Orchard*
Highbank Orchards*
Kilmegan Irish Cider*
Llewellyns Orchard*
Long Meadow Cider*
Longueville House Cider*

Mac Ivors Cider
Mac's Armagh Cider*
Orpens
Stonewell Irish Craft Cider*
Tempted? Irish Craft Cider*
The Apple Farm*
Toby's Handcrafted Cider*

Member of Cider Ireland

Orchard tours

As of September 2014, all Cider Ireland members are either open to visitors or plan on being so in the near future. If you would like to visit one of the orchards, give them a ring to see if they might be able to show you around. You can also catch up with the producers at one of the many festivals throughout the year.

Armagh Cider Company

Portadown, Co. Armagh | www.armaghcider.com

Apples run deep in Philip and Helen Troughton's blood – they are fourth-generation apple-growers at Ballinteggart House, outside Portadown, where the Troughton family has been growing apples since 1898. Their ciders – Carsons Crisp Armagh Cider, a traditional cider, and Maddens Mellow Armagh Cider, a slightly sweeter cider – are made with apples grown on the home farm and pressed in a traditional rack and cloth press. Their Molly's Mulled Armagh Cider just needs to be poured into a pot and gently heated on the stove for a perfect autumn pick-me-up after a brisk walk. Their product range also extends to pure apple juice, a non-alcoholic apple punch and cider vinegar. They use their own Armagh Bramley apples in their blossom-to-bottle ciders, so they are allowed to use the PGI logo. Visitors are welcome to tour the orchards and cidery – a particularly special treat when the trees are in bloom in the spring.

Ciders: Carsons Crisp Armagh Cider, Maddens Mellow Armagh Cider, Molly's Mulled Armagh Cider

The Cider Mill

Slane, Co. Meath | www.cockagee.ie

If you had to sum up The Cider Mill in one word, that word would be *traditional*. Mark Jenkinson is inspired by an old heritage Irish apple variety, the Cockagee, that had a reputation for making excellent cider (see page 70 for more). He takes things one step further by using a cider-making technique called keeving, a centuries-old way of making naturally sweet, softly sparkling cider, to produce his unique product – the only keeved cider in Ireland. It is a 100% natural, 'live' cider. It hasn't been filtered, pasteurised, back sweetened or force carbonated – the sweetness and sparkle are due to the actions of natural yeasts in the cider. This award-winning boutique cider is one for true aficionados and is well worth seeking out – think of it as an Irish alternative to champagne.

Cider: Cockagee Pure Irish Keeved Cider

Craigies Irish Cider
Grangecon, Co. Wicklow | www.craigiescider.ie

What does a wine specialist with twenty years' experience in the industry and a diploma in wine production do? Start a cider-making business, of course! It's not as much of a stretch as it might first seem. Faced with a lack of vines in Ireland but an abundance of apples, Simon Tyrrell teamed up with farmer Angus Craigie in

2011 to produce a classic medium-dry cider, Ballyhook Flyer, on Angus's farm. Simon concentrates on the fermentation side of things while Angus looks after the processing and logistics end. 'While the craft cider movement owes a lot to the craft beer movement, in reality it has much more in common with wine,' Simon explains. 'Many beers are brewed all year round and to the same recipe, whereas most cider is made once a year and is subject to all the vagaries of the climate in that year. For us it's important to show these vintage variations, and to talk about the specifics of each orchard and what makes the apples that come from them so special.' They added a second cider, Dalliance, made entirely from dessert apples, in 2014, but we love the inspiration behind the name of their flagship cider – the original Ballyhook Flyer that was entered in the Grangecon Soapbox Derby and a self-styled west Wicklow legend. For now, their cider is made with 100% Irish apples from Waterford, Tipperary and Kilkenny until their own orchards bear fruit.

Ciders: Ballyhook Flyer, Dalliance

Dan Kelly's Cider
Drogheda, Co. Louth | www.dankellyscider.com

Boyne Grove Fruit Farm is a family business to the core – their farm manager, Henry Mallon, has seen four generations work on the farm, and the fifth is on its way. Olan, Fiona and John Paul McNeece, a brothers-and-sister team, are the latest in a long line of apple-growers. Their great-grandfather planted a Bramley orchard on his small farm in Co. Armagh in the late 1890s, and their grandfather went on to buy his own farm in 1933, also in Armagh. Their father, Gerry, bought their current orchard in Drogheda, Co. Louth, in 1962 (from the local Cairnes brewing family, coincidentally enough). They currently produce one cider, Dan Kelly's Cider, named after their great-grandfather on their father's mother's side, who drove the Dublin–Belfast train that runs through the farm. It is made from a blend of their own hand-picked Bramleys and

dessert apples and wild yeasts. They also plan to develop single varietals and vintage ciders, and are hoping to be open for visits and tours of the cider-making facility in the future. One to watch.

Cider: Dan Kelly's Cider

Dovehill Orchard

Carrick-on-Suir, Co. Tipperary

Never one to pass up a challenge, in 1997 James O'Donoghue got involved in a Bulmers pilot project to grow Dabinett and Michelin cider apples – despite the fact that he didn't have any land. A few months later, he purchased a farm and 1998 saw him planting his first apple trees. That initial 20-acre planting has since been joined by another 6 acres of cider apples, and James is now concentrating on managing his orchard and harvest methods to produce a cider that reflects his specific *terroir*. The Dovehill Orchard Medium Dry is the first cider to market and a lightly carbonated  table cider is in development, which he intends to be a viable Irish alternative to white wine.

Cider: Dovehill Orchard Medium Dry Cider

Highbank Orchards

Cuffesgrange, Co. Kilkenny | www.highbankorchards.com

Highbank Orchards are most well known for their award-winning Highbank Orchard Syrup, Ireland's home-grown answer to maple syrup. But Rod and Julie Calder-Potts are nothing if not innovative, and their organic seventeenth-century farm has also produced apple juice, hops and, as of 2012, cider. Theirs is the only certified organic cider in Ireland and they currently make four distinct versions, all of which have been developed to go with food: the Highbank Proper Cider, made with their own organic cider apples and wild yeast; Highbank Medieval Cider, which is a variation of their Proper Cider but with organic honey added to it; Highbank Dessert Cider, a sweet blend designed to be served with cheese or to round off the end of a meal; and Driver's Cider, a sparkling non-alcoholic cider. They only produce small batches, so keep your eye out for it and snap it up whenever you see it – their own farm shop is a good bet.

Ciders: Highbank Dessert Cider, Highbank Driver's Cider (non-alcoholic), Highbank Medieval Cider, Highbank Proper Cider

Kilmegan Irish Cider

Dundrum, Co. Down | www.kilmegancider.com

The origins of Kilmegan Irish Cider sound like something out of a fairytale: in 1967, Andrew Boyd's father discovered a seventy-year-old orchard hidden underneath a six-metre-high wall of brambles next to the farmhouse he and his wife had bought in the shadow of the Mourne Mountains. Andrew grew up eating those apples, but fast forward to 2009, when he and his own wife threw some fresh-pressed apple juice and champagne yeast into a demijohn, stuck on an airlock and came back a few months later to find cider. These days they use a traditional apple mill and a rack and  cloth press to make their range of ciders, still using apples from Andrew's father's small orchard – a true farmhouse cider. Their cider infused with wild elderflowers is a particularly special summertime treat.

Ciders: Kilmegan Irish Farmhouse Cider, Kilmegan Real Cider, Kilmegan Wild Elderflower-Infused Cider

Rod and Julie Calder-Potts from Highbank Orchards

Llewellyns Orchard
Lusk, Co. Dublin | www.llewellynsorchard.ie

David Llewellyn is a man on a mission: he wants to educate people as to what true cider actually is and how good and wholesome it is. When he started testing the market with his cider in 2001, he was the only person in the Republic who was selling the real deal and had an immediate, if small, following of customers who had tasted proper cider abroad. Even though there are many new craft ciders available now, David's is still unique in that he uses a natural secondary bottle fermentation to give it sparkle rather than carbonating it, and his cider isn't filtered or pasteurised  either. David's two mainstay ciders are the Bone Dry and Medium Dry versions, made with a blend of three different kinds of Irish apples, but his single-varietal Katy Reserve 2011 won a Pomme d'Or award at the 2014 International Cider Fair. David also runs cider-making courses in the autumn, so be sure to check his website or contact him for details of dates and locations.

Ciders: Double L Bone Dry Cider, Double L Medium Dry Cider, Katy Reserve

Long Meadow Cider
Portadown, Co. Armagh | www.longmeadowcider.com

Long Meadow Cider is produced by father and son duo Pat and Peter McKeever in the heart of Ireland's Orchard County, where their family-run business has been growing apples for fifty years. Talking to the *Portadown Times*, Pat said making cider was a natural progression when they decided to diversify back in 2010. 'We were growing apples for the processing and packaging markets and also supplying apples to a number of cider-producing companies in the South and thought it would be nice if we could start producing our own brand of cider and so we started looking into that.' They now produce two ciders – a medium and a sweet – made exclusively from their own apples and using traditional methods.

Ciders: Medium Cider, Sweet Cider

Longueville House Cider
Mallow, Co. Cork | www.longuevillehouse.ie

The Longueville House estate has many strings in its bow: a renowned country house hotel with their own lamb, salmon, fruit and vegetables and wine (yes, wine!), as well as Ireland's only apple brandy and cider made from their own apples. The late Michael O'Callaghan originally developed the cider as a means to an end to make the brandy (which is made by distilling the cider in pot stills and then ageing it in French oak barrels for four years), but for the past few years his son, William, has been developing the cider as a standout product in its own right. Longueville House hosts an annual Harvest Lunch and Cider-Making Tour in the autumn if you want to see where the magic happens.

Cider: Longueville House Cider

Mac Ivors Cider
Portadown, Co. Armagh | www.macivors.com

Greg MacNiece's mother is French and her family are wine-growers, and after drinking the renowned French ciders he wondered why we couldn't get similar cider here in Ireland – a natural enough question for a fifth-generation apple-grower. So he set out to make it himself. Mac Ivors is made from hand-picked, fresh-pressed apples from their own 100-acre family orchard in Co. Armagh, as well as neighbouring orchards. 'Cider is all about the sum of its parts,' says Greg, and it all comes down to the raw materials: the fruit.

Ciders: Traditional Dry Cider, Medium Cider

Mac's Armagh Cider

Forkhill, Co. Armagh

Founded in 1995 when Seán Mac an tSaoir planted two cider apple orchards, Mac's is the granddaddy of the Irish cider revival. As the first maker of craft cider, Seán had to retrain people to appreciate proper cider as opposed to the 'apple alcopops' that the larger manufacturers were producing. Seán grew up in the Orchard County and has 'been interested in craft brewing forever'. 'Blending is the real art,' he says, 'which only those with a true appreciation for cider can master, and it takes time to develop your understanding of the variability from season to season. The drier the cider, the greater the challenge. And there is no shortcut for this bit – time has to be served.' He produces four ciders, using apples only from Armagh: Mac's 401 Belfast Scrumpy, a traditional scrumpy-style cider; Mac's Dry Cider, an unapologetically dry cider (he calls it the black coffee equivalent of cider); Mac's Sweet Cider, which has added sugar and reduced tannin levels to create a more middle-of-the-road cider; and Mac's Lyte, a tribute to the French tradition of low alcohol cider that you can drink with your lunch and still carry on working, and which won the first All-Ireland Cider Competition at the Armagh Agricultural Show in 2011. Seán operates under the 70hl limit for paying duty, so the ciders can be hard to find, but they are well worth tracking down.

Ciders: Mac's 401 Belfast Scrumpy, Mac's Dry Cider, Mac's Lyte, Mac's Sweet Cider

Orpens

www.orpens.ie

What do you get when you put two sons of Irish apple-growers and a South African winemaker with a cider-maker grandfather together? One award-winning cider that aspires to wine's pedigree. Orpens is a collaboration between Irishmen Chris Hill and Matt Tindal and South African Bruce Jack, who travels to Ireland once a month to do the blending. All three come from a wine background, which is immediately apparent when they talk about their cider and the philosophy behind it. Their conversation is shot through with words

like *vintage*, *elegance*, *balance* and *finesse* and they talk of making a cider with a clean, pure profile with the fruit to the fore, balanced with just the right mix of tannins, acidity and sugar, that can be enjoyed with or without food. The Troughtons of Armagh Cider Company originally made Orpens Cider, but these days it's made at the C&C plant in Clonmel and is available throughout Ireland and even the UK too.

Cider: Orpens Handcrafted Irish Cider

Stonewell Irish Craft Cider
Kinsale, Co. Cork | www.stonewellcider.com

There is an old walled garden on Daniel Emerson's small farm in Nohoval that includes an orchard with about forty trees. Daniel says that there is only so much apple pie and stewed apple that you can get into a chest freezer, so his father bought a tabletop apple press and they started making cider for family and friends. Jumping ahead a few years, Daniel's French father-in-law, a winemaker from the Loire Valley, gifted Daniel an old basket press and apple scratter. Their production shot up to about 1,000 litres of cider a year after that – more than enough for all their family and friends, with plenty left over. They used the old French press to develop their first blends, but they quickly outgrew it. They continue to use traditional methods and all-natural ingredients and they source apples solely from Irish orchards in the apple-growing areas of Tipperary, Cork, Kilkenny and Waterford. And except for the glass bottles, everything about a Stonewell cider is Irish – the apples, the labels, the cartons and, of course, the elbow grease! Stonewell was the winner of the inaugural Irish Food Writers' Guild Drink Award in 2014 – try the cider sorbet that Michelin-starred chef Derry Clarke created in honour of their win (see page 194).

Ciders: Stonewell Dry Craft Cider, Stonewell Medium Dry Craft Cider, Stonewell Tobairín Cider (low-alcohol)

Tempted? Irish Craft Cider
Lisburn, Co. Antrim | www.temptedcider.com

When Davy Uprichard asked himself what grew locally to him in Northern Ireland and what could be made from it that he would like to eat or drink, the answer was clear: apples and cider. Before that, Davy had studied horticulture at Queen's University in Belfast, had his own plant nursery business and had learned how to make wine with his father, Jim, so it's easy to see how cider sprang to mind. Four award-winning ciders are made: Dry, Davy's original cider; Summer Sweet, which is given a boost from Davy's own pure pressed apple juice; Strawberry, a blend of sweet cider, apple juice and the strawberry wine Davy developed with his father; and Special Reserve, which has a more complex flavour. Tempted? cider is made in a purpose-built cidery at Davy's home outside Lisburn, and his dream has become a business that now involves the whole family.

Ciders: Medium Dry, Special Reserve, Strawberry, Summer Sweet

The Apple Farm
Cahir, Co. Tipperary | www.theapplefarm.com

Con Traas's fruit-growing business is a family affair that was established by his parents in the 1960s when they moved from the Netherlands to Tipperary. Con himself studied Agricultural Science in UCD before bringing his knowledge back to the land. He grows a wide variety of apples – almost fifty types at last count – for eating, juicing and now, cider-making. While this is a relatively recent move, he has been the go-to guy for cider producers throughout Ireland for many years. Writing in the *Sunday Business Post*, Tomás Clancy called him 'a gravitational force around which many artisan cider producers orbit', as Con offers a contract apple pressing and bottling service that many start-up cider-makers have availed of. Con's Irish Cider, blended from the unique Karmijn de Sonnaville apple (Con is the only grower in Ireland), along with Jonagold, Bramley and Dabinett, will undoubtedly see him making his mark in the artisan cider sector.

Cider: Con's Irish Cider

Toby's Handcrafted Cider

Portadown, Co. Armagh | www.tobyscider.co.uk

Craig and Karen Shipman had been making cider for friends and family for years before they started to sell it to the public in 2008. All the apples that go into Toby's cider are grown on their own orchards or within walking distance of the farm, and when they say it's a handcrafted cider, they mean it. Everything is done by hand – the apples are hand picked, graded by hand and washed by hand, and the cider is even bottled by hand by their small family team and a few friends who help out at the busy times of year. Their attention to detail paid off when they won the gold award for the best international cider at the Wales Perry and Cider Scoiety Championships in May 2014. A percentage from every bottle of Toby's Cider sold is donated to the Toby Fund, which was set up to raise funds to help sick children – a good cider for a good cause.

Cider: Toby's Handcrafted Katy Cider (sweet), Toby's Handcrafted Original Cider (dry)

CHAPTER 6

MATCHING BEER AND CIDER WITH FOOD

There has been a renaissance in the Irish artisan food movement, so it's not surprising to see Irish craft brewing and cider production gathering pace alongside it. Speaking at the launch of the tenth edition of the *Irish Food Guide* in 2012, food writer John McKenna of the *McKennas' Guides* singled out craft brewers as one of three key drivers of the success of the artisan food sector, the other two being free-range, rare-breed pigs and sourdough bread. Remember how beer and bread saved civilisation in Chapter 2? Maybe it could do the same for the Irish economy.

Beoir agus Bia

Did you know that beer is actually a better match with food than wine? We like a glass of crisp white wine with seafood or a full-bodied red with a steak as much as the next person, but beer simply ticks more boxes and shines where wine falls short.

- Hops stimulate the appetite due to their bitter taste, making beer an ideal drink to have with a meal.
- The bubbly, cleansing carbonation in beer gives a refreshing lift to your palate, leaving you ready to taste each bite like it's the first. This is especially true for rich, fatty foods and cheese. This 'scrubbing bubbles' action also has the effect of lightening up the meal.
- Beer has a greater range of flavours than wine. Wine is restricted by its single ingredient – grapes – but beer can play with different variations of grains, hops and yeast and other add-ins like spices, chocolate, chillies, nuts, fruit or vegetables. The greater flavour range in the drink means that there are more opportunities to find equivalent matches (or contrasts) with the food.

> 'Wine is but single broth, ale is meat, drink, and cloth.'
> – Sixteenth-century English proverb

Ireland became a nation of wine drinkers during the Celtic Tiger. Wine sales quadrupled from 1990 to 2007, but they plummeted, along with everything else, in the crash. As Dwight D. Eisenhower said, 'Some people wanted champagne and caviar when they should have had beer and hot dogs.'

Wine writers have had the field all to themselves for decades, telling us how to match it with food or pair it with cheese, even though beer does a better job at both. In *The Brewmaster's Table*, Garrett Oliver writes that wine is a poor substitute for beer when it comes to food. 'Why? Because spices distort wine flavours, turning white wines hot and red wines bitter. Because wine doesn't refresh the palate the way beer does. Because wine has no caramelised or roasted flavours to match those in our favourite dishes. And because, even according to wine experts, there are many foods that are simply no good with wine.' In short, 'beer leaps in where wine fears to tread'.

Food-Friendly Beer

With beer and food matching becoming ever more popular, you hear a lot about food-friendly beer these days. In Belgium they have a name for this kind of beer: *tafelbier, bière de table* or 'table beer', which has a low ABV (1% to 4%), a light body and is meant to be served with meals. Closer to home, White Gypsy's 75cl bottles of speciality beers have been specifically brewed to accompany food.

A food-friendly beer is a Goldilocks kind of beer: not too bitter, not too strong, not too alcoholic. But that doesn't mean it will be a boring beer – quite the opposite. A multidimensional, flavourful beer with complex character provides more hooks for the food to latch onto and means it can partner with a number of different dishes. The most successful matches bring out the best in the food *and* the beer; the best matches are nothing short of magic.

Top Tips for Matching Beer and Food

Now that the Irish craft beer industry is booming, there is more selection than ever before. The range of flavours and the versatility of craft beer mean that there is a match for just about any food, from chilli to chocolate, curry to Christmas dinner. Matching beer and food is not an exact science, but there are some general guidelines you can follow to get the best out of both of them.

1. **Complement or contrast?** This is the first thing to decide when matching beer with food. Do you want to highlight the similar flavours in the beer and food, or do you want to use their differences to contrast them instead? For example, a hoppy IPA can complement a spicy curry or contrast with rich, smoked meat, while an earthy stout complements chocolate but is also a classic contrast to the delicate, briny sweetness of oysters.

2. **Pair like with like.** A good rule of thumb is that delicate beers go well with delicate foods. Think wheat beers and blonde ales with seafood – a strong, dark beer would overwhelm those light flavours. Those same strong beers are a natural match for heartier dishes though, such as stout or red ale with roasts and stews.

3. **Pace your flavours.** If you are matching different beers to different courses of a meal, start with the lighter-flavoured beers and progress to the bigger, bolder beers, not the other way around, otherwise the stronger beers will overpower the lighter ones.

4. **Think seasonally.** Lawnmower beers are called that for a good reason. You naturally want a crisp pilsner as a refreshing lift when the sun is blazing, while an earthy stout is just the thing for sipping by a crackling fire in the pub on a cold winter's day. It follows, then, that those same styles are often a good match for seasonal dishes. A lager is great with a summer barbecue, while a porter is perfect for autumn game.

5. **Translate your favourite wine style into beer.** If you already know what wine styles you like or what wines you like with food, you can roughly translate them into a beer style. If you like light-bodied wines such as Sauvignon Blanc or Pinot Grigio, go for a lager, pilsner or wheat beer. If you would have served a medium-bodied wine like Merlot, Zinfandel or Syrah, opt for an ale or IPA. Or if you prefer Cabernet Sauvignon, Syrah or Malbec, try a stout, porter or dubbel.

Beer and Food Matching Cheat Sheet

Here are some quick guidelines for matching common styles of craft beer and cider to food. If you remember this general rule of thumb, you won't go wrong: lighter, more delicate dishes pair well with similarly light beers, while bolder flavours need a darker, more full-bodied or more bitter beer to stand up to them. Or to be somewhat simplistic, light-coloured food generally goes well with light-coloured beer and dark-coloured food goes well with dark-coloured beer.

Blonde ale	Chicken, seafood
British bitter	Bangers and mash, chicken (roasted or fried), game, ham, ploughman's lunch, pork, roasted red meat, seafood, shepherd's pie, Thai food
Brown ale	BBQ, cured meat, game, mushrooms, ploughman's lunch, pork, red meat, steak, stews
Cider	Apple desserts, curry, pork, sausages
Fruit beers	Cheesecake, chocolate, duck, goose, Mexican mole sauce, panna cotta, venison
IPA	Game, smoked fish or meat, spicy food, Mexican food, Thai food, Vietnamese food
Lager	BBQ, burgers, chicken, pizza, seafood, Mexican food, mildly spicy food
Lambics	Blue cheese, charcuterie, goat's cheese, oysters and seafood, salads, sausages
Red ale	Bacon and cabbage, BBQ, burgers, chicken, lamb, pork, pizza, steak or any roasted or grilled meats
Pale ale	Burgers, cold meats, creamy pasta sauces, grilled meat, roast beef, roast chicken, pâté, ploughman's lunch, quiche, Thai food
Pilsner	Asian food, chicken, chowder, ham, Indian food, salads, seafood, spicy food, Thai food
Stout and porter	Bacon, beef, berries, black pudding, burgers, braised dishes, chocolate, corned beef, game, ham, lamb, meatloaf, oysters, roasted and smoked food, salty food, scallops, shepherd's pie, steak, stew
Trappist and abbey-style ales	**Dubbels:** beef stew, black pudding, duck, lamb, roast chicken, sausages, steak. **Tripels:** asparagus, game birds, ham, oily fish, pesto, sausages
Wheat beer	Brunch, grilled chicken, Indian food, Mexican food, mussels, pork, salads, seafood, Thai food

Beer and BBQ

Because barbecued food has so much flavour, you want a beer that not only stands up to the food, but enhances it too.

- **Burgers:** Pale ales, IPAs and brown ales are great with the meaty intensity of a burger.
- **Chicken:** A red or brown ale will complement the charred flavours of barbecued chicken.
- **Pork:** The caramelised malt in red ales is a good pairing for the sweetness in grilled pork, especially sausages. Or try a crisp, cold craft cider – apples and pork have a natural affinity for each other and cider is a favourite summertime drink.
- **Seafood:** Lighter beers like a wheat beer, pilsner or blonde ale are good choices for more delicately flavoured seafood.

If you are slathering everything with the same barbecue sauce, which will probably be both sweet and acidic, then a crisp lager would be a good overall choice and is always a popular beer at barbecues. Steer clear of very hoppy IPAs though – the flavours of the barbecue sauce and the beer will compete with each other instead of contrast or complement.

Beer and Chocolate

Beer and chocolate probably isn't the first pairing that springs to mind, but they are a beautiful match. 'No wine can match chocolate desserts nearly as well as the right beer,' writes Garrett Oliver in *The Brewmaster's Table*.

Stout and porter are the perfect partners for chocolate and chocolate desserts. It's a case of complementing the common flavours to pick up on the toasted, roasted and bitter flavours in each of them. The roasted malts in stouts and porters often naturally lend coffee and chocolate flavours to the beer as well.

Alternatively, just as fresh cherries and raspberries are wonderful with chocolate, so too are sweet fruit lambics such as a kriek or framboise. And don't forget white chocolate – IPAs, Belgian-style blonde ales and tripels are all potential matches.

> *'Dost thou think, because thou art virtuous, there shall be no more cakes and ale?'*
>
> – *William Shakespeare*, Twelfth Night

Cakes and ale

There is more to pairing beer and baked goods than chocolate and stout (though that is always a winner). With advice from beer bloggers John Duffy and Reuben Gray, as well as Derek Pearce from the Celtic Whiskey Shop, baker Caryna Camerino (www.carynascakes.com) hosted an evening of cake and Irish craft beer pairings in 2013, which all went down a treat.

- Lime Coconut Macaroon Cake with a Thyme-Infused Clara con Limón Made with Dungarvan Helvick Gold
- Chilli Chocolate Tart with O'Hara's Leann Folláin Extra Irish Stout
- Peanut Caramel Brownie with Dungarvan Copper Coast Irish Red Ale
- French Crêpes and Rhubarb Apple Compote with Mac's Armagh Cider
- Baked Vanilla Bean Cheesecake with White Gypsy Dubbel

Beer and Ethnic Food

Any country's cuisine covers a huge spectrum of flavours and ingredients, so it is impossible to provide an exhaustive list of food and beer matches here. Remember the principle that lighter beers work well with light, delicately flavoured food and darker beers match well with heavier, meatier food and you won't go too far wrong.

Chinese

From crispy roasted duck to fresh spring rolls wrapped in rice paper, there is a beer to complement any Chinese dish the next time you find yourself at the takeaway. If you want one beer that will likely work well with everyone's different choices, try a wheat beer.

- Have a wheat beer or pilsner with fresh (not fried) spring rolls, delicate noodle dishes or dim sum.
- If you're having a deep-fried dish, pick a palate-cleansing lager, blonde ale or märzen.
- The roasted flavours in stouts and strong, dark ales work well with roasted or barbecued meats, especially something like pork in a plum sauce.

- A rich duck dish would be beautifully offset by a fruit beer or a strong, sweet ale.
- A sweet, malty ale or stout can be a good contrast to salty soy sauce or oyster sauce. Conversely, they can also complement a hoisin sauce. Or if you prefer lighter beer, try a blonde ale or red ale, especially with milder chicken dishes.
- If you can get your hands on a smoked beer, try it with a sesame oil-based dish. Otherwise, try a stout that has particularly smoky, earthy undertones.

Curry

Curry and beer is a classic match – the carbonation and hop bitterness in beer work wonders when put up against a spicy curry. The bubbles provide a much-needed lift and cleanse your palate, while the hop bitterness cuts through the spiciness in a curry, both in terms of flavour and heat. A word of warning, though: if you love fiery hot curries, keep an eye on the alcohol level of whatever beer you match with it. The higher the ABV, the hotter it makes the heat!

IPAs and lagers tend to be the most popular pairings with a curry, but blonde ales, pilsners and wheat beers can work too. Try these:

- A hoppy IPA with a highly spiced curry
- Blonde ale, lager or wheat beer with a chicken tikka masala
- Wheat beer with a creamy korma
- Pilsner or golden ale with a rogan josh

Mexican

The flavours in Mexican food range from a simple dish of beans and rice to rich, robust mole sauces. If you are looking for one all-purpose beer, a lager or wheat beer would be your best bet. Otherwise, there is plenty of scope to experiment with more nuanced pairings.

- The same principles that apply to matching beer and curry apply to spicy Mexican food. As such, it's hard to beat lager or IPA.
- Try a malty beer, such as a red ale, to cut through the cheese and earthy cumin spice in quesadillas, enchiladas, burritos, fajitas and tacos. If the dish has chicken as the star ingredient, try a lighter beer like a pilsner, lager or wheat beer instead. IPAs and stouts can also be successful matches, depending on the filling.

- Mole sauces pair particularly well with a dry kriek, framboise or a dunkelweizen (dark wheat beer), while red chilli adobo sauces would work well with a strong ale.

> 'Never underestimate how much assistance, how much satisfaction, how much comfort, how much soul and transcendence there might be in a well-made taco and a cold bottle of beer.'
> – Tom Robbins, Jitterbug Perfume

Thai

Thai food is renowned for its fresh, clean flavours. Ginger, lemongrass, lime, chilli, coconut and fish sauce are some of the hallmarks. A slightly sour lambic or gueuze is a surprisingly good contrast, as is a simple pilsner, while the lemony spritz of a wheat beer or the hoppiness of a pale ale or British bitter are good complements to that same brightness in Thai dishes.

Beer and Meat

Beef

Beer's hoppy bitterness is a good contrast for the richness of beef, while its roasted and caramelised malt flavours complement those same flavours in roasted or chargrilled beef, such as a well-seared steak. You need a strong, earthy beer with a heavier body to stand up to beef's bold flavour. Strong ales and malty beers like stouts, porters and brown ales are good contenders. If you can, try to pick a beer that has a sharper, hoppy edge, as opposed to one that is on the sweet side, to play up the contrast between the beef and the beer.

Chicken and turkey

There are as many ways to prepare chicken as there are days in the year, but generally speaking you will need a lighter beer to avoid overpowering what is essentially a fairly bland meat (the same goes for turkey). A pale ale or a crisp, clean blonde ale would work just as well with a roast chicken or turkey as it would with fried chicken, while a red ale is a good match for barbecued chicken. If you want to complement the roasted flavours of a turkey, serve a malty red ale, brown ale or a dubbel.

Duck

Duck is another good example of why beer and food go so well together. The palate-cleansing carbonation of the beer slices through the rich, fatty meat, while fruit beers pick up on the same flavours in duck served with a sweet glaze or fruit sauce.

- **Confit or cassoulet:** Brown ale, dubbel, doppelbock, fruit beers or lambics, strong pale ale
- **Duck with a sweet glaze or fruit sauce:** Fruit beer, porter, stout
- **Roast duck:** Dubbel, doppelbock or a strong, dark ale
- **Smoked duck:** IPA
- **Spicy duck:** IPA, pale ale, pilsner

Game

The strong, pronounced flavours of wild game need a beer that can hold its own against the meat. Stouts and porters are the first thing that come to mind here, but dubbels, strong ales, brown ales and British bitters fit the bill too.

Lamb

Stout is a good match for lamb, as each have slightly earthy flavours. If you are roasting the lamb, like a traditional leg of lamb studded with rosemary and garlic, serve a strong pale ale for a nice contrast or a red ale to complement the caramelised flavours in the roast. Lamb burgers hold their own when matched with a heartier beer, so try a strong ale or Belgian-style ale, brown ale or a stout or porter. Lamb with a mint sauce, on the other hand, would work well with a lighter, zippier beer, such as a pilsner.

> In February 2014, Conwy Brewery in Wales launched its Sunday Toast ale, infused with the juices from slow-roasted lamb, to celebrate St David's Day. Irish stew beer, anyone?

Pork

When matching pork and beer, it's all about the sweetness of the pork. A red ale, dubbel, doppelbock, märzen and mild lambics or fruit beers are all good options. Ham would benefit from being paired with pilsner, märzen, strong golden ale or stout, while sausages are happy to be paired with pretty much any beer. And don't forget that pork and cider are a beautiful match too (see pages 140–141).

Beer and Pasta

It is undoubtedly more traditional to serve wine with pasta, but that doesn't mean that matching beer and pasta won't work. To decide on a match, it might help to think of it in wine terms – if it is a dish you would normally have with white wine, choose a lighter, spritzy beer; if you would drink a red wine with it, serve a darker, heartier beer.

- **Cream or cheese sauce:** A heavier, richer beer will stand up to a cream or cheese sauce – try a strong ale or doppelbock. If you would rather go the lighter route, try a wheat beer. A pale ale that isn't too bitter will also work well.
- **Meat sauce:** A brown ale or pale ale will counteract the richness of the meat.
- **Pesto:** Try a strong golden ale or a tripel with a herby pesto.
- **Seafood:** You don't want to overwhelm delicately flavoured seafood, so try a wheat beer, blonde ale or pilsner. If it is a spicy seafood sauce, try an IPA. For heartier shellfish, such as lobsters, crabs, mussels or clams, try a stout.
- **Tomato sauce:** A red ale or brown ale will counteract the acidity of a tomato sauce while also complementing its slight sweetness.

Beer and Pizza

It stands to reason that just as beer and cheese is a match made in heaven, so is beer and pizza. The carbonation in beer cuts through the fat in cheese and scrubs your palate clean, and of course the yeasty, bready flavours in beer pick up on the same flavours in the pizza dough.

With such a limitless range of toppings, it is hard to suggest definitive beer and pizza pairings. A good rule of thumb is that plainer pizzas, such as a simple margherita, go well with lighter beers, but as you start to pile on the toppings, you'll need a stronger-flavoured beer to keep up.

- A biscuity, bready pilsner or an Oktoberfest märzen pair well with plainer pizzas, complementing the bread base without being overwhelmed by toppings. Any light lager is a good all-round choice here.
- The malty, caramel, slightly sweet flavours in a red ale balance well with a tomato sauce and also help to neutralise its acidity. A fruity red ale is also a good match if your toppings include sausage or bacon.
- Just as a pale ale and a spicy curry are a classic combination, try a pale ale with a spicy pizza – its hop bitterness will cut through the spiciness, both in terms of flavour and heat.

- A stout or porter will work well with a particularly salty pizza, such as an anchovy pizza, a salty and sweet *pissaldiere* (a Provençal pizza/tart with olives, onions and anchovies) or a pizza with blue cheese.

If you make your own pizza at home, try swapping out some of the water in the pizza dough for beer to add an extra dimension of flavour. Just remember that the stronger the beer you use, the more pronounced the flavour will be in the dough – which is no bad thing.

Beer and Vegetables

Meat hogs the limelight when it comes to matching beer and food, but there are plenty of great pairings with vegetables and vegetarian dishes too. Remember the rule of thumb when matching any beer and food – light beers with light flavours; darker, stronger beers with stronger flavours – and you'll be off to a good start.

- Salads and steamed or sautéed vegetables go well with lighter beers, such as a pilsner, blonde ale, lager or wheat beer.
- Roasting or grilling vegetables brings out their inherent sweetness, especially root vegetables, and develops a smoky, chargrilled flavour, so pair them with malty beers with a little caramel sweetness of their own, such as a red ale, brown ale, märzen or a light porter. Cider is also a good match for roasted veg (see page 141).
- Onions' sharp bite will get a bite back from a hoppy pale ale. If the onions are roasted or caramelised, try complementing their sweetness with a red ale, brown ale or porter, as with other roasted veg dishes.
- Give spicy vegetable dishes extra oomph by serving a hoppy IPA alongside.
- Mushrooms, which are full of umami, can handle a hoppy beer like a strong ale, but their earthiness pairs well with darker beers like doppelbock, porter or a brown ale too.
- A beer to *avoid* with vegetables is any beer that is especially bitter, as the beer will unpleasantly accentuate any inherent bitterness in the vegetables.

'For a quart of ale is a dish for a king.'
– William Shakespeare, A Winter's Tale

Beer and Seafood

The key thing to remember when matching seafood and beer is that seafood is less robust than other meaty dishes, so you need to pick a beer that won't overwhelm its lighter, more delicate flavours. Good beer styles to match with a wide range of seafood are wheat beer (especially shellfish), blonde ale and pilsner. An IPA is a good match for smoked fish, spicy seafood dishes like prawns pil pil or deep-fried fish like a classic fish 'n' chips, where the hoppy bitterness cuts through the oiliness. A stout is a classic match for oysters, but it also matches well with the sweetness of lobsters, scallops, crab, mussels and calamari too.

Stout and oysters

A pint of stout and a dozen oysters is one of life's little luxuries. We now think of stout and oysters as an upscale, elegant pairing, but the origins of this match are quite humble. In the eighteenth and nineteenth centuries, oysters were food for the working classes. It was only when oyster beds started to become exhausted towards the beginning of the twentieth century, as a result of which oysters became scarcer and more expensive, that they became the delicacy we think of them as today.

At the same time as the oyster beds were flourishing, so was stout and the two were often served together in pubs and taverns as a cheap and cheerful meal or bar snack. The bitter, roasted, smooth flavour of a dry Irish stout is a beautiful contrast to the creamy, salty, sweet oysters. 'One can almost imagine the beer as the knife that cracks the oyster open – there seems to be a primal connection between them. The flavour of the oyster is magically magnified and fills the senses,' writes Garrett Oliver in *The Brewmaster's Table*.

And then there are oyster stouts. This can refer either to a beer designed to be sipped alongside oysters or to a stout with oysters added directly to it. Some brewers just use the shells (as a clarifying agent), while others add the oyster itself. The result is often a barely discernible brininess and a more full-bodied mouthfeel from the protein in the oyster. Try one for yourself and see – Porterhouse makes an oyster stout, with fresh oysters shucked directly into the conditioning tank.

L. Mulligan Grocer: 'A Dream of a Gastropub'

New York Times writer Rosie Schaap called L. Mulligan Grocer 'a dream of a gastropub' when she visited Dublin in 2012. Two years later, her fellow *NYT* writer David Farley said that they were 'serving some of the most exciting food in Dublin' in his 2014 write-up of Dublin's dining scene.

Opened in July 2010 by Seáneen Sullivan, Colin Hession and Michael Fogarty, the team combined their respective passions for food, craft beer and whiskey to build something special in Stoneybatter. 'Mulligan's is a very old pub, so we see ourselves as custodians of a long tradition of eating and drinking here,' Seáneen says. And yet they also wanted to offer something different from all the other pubs on the street, which all sold the same big-brand beers. 'We wanted to do something exceptional – we made no secret of that,' she continues. 'We wanted to create a pub that we would like to eat in, drink in, socialise in. We wanted to create something at the heart of the community that we are proud to be a part of.'

They were amongst the first champions of Irish craft beer (and craft beer in general) and were famously the first pub in the capital not to serve Guinness. They also have the biggest selection of cask beer in the city. 'We are passionate about cask. We have seven handpumps, we source casks directly from the UK and also ask kindly for many local breweries to cask for us. We also bought our own casks, so we can give these to the likes of David Llewellyn or the lovely lads at Barrelhead to fill with craft beer/cider.'

They also pioneered beer and food matching in Ireland. They pair all the dishes on their menu with a suggested beer, and they regularly host special beer and food matching dinners. 'I remember catering a party long before we opened LMG, a five-course beer dinner,' Seáneen says. 'People were amazed beer and food could work so well together. It's great to be able to be a part of that realisation. We are very lucky that we get to do that every day.'

We asked Seáneen to share some of the L. Mulligan Grocer team's favourite beer and food pairings. Try them for yourself the next time you are in the restaurant or use them to inspire you for your own beer and food matches at home.

1. Brown Paper Bag Project Gøse with freshly shucked oysters

2. Rodenbach Grand Cru with 'Sir' Jack McCarthy's black pudding, apple and red onion boxty, beetroot purée, pickled cherries and port reduction

3. Franciscan Well Jameson Barrel-Aged Stout with dark chocolate cake, cherries, hazelnuts and sea salt crumb

4. Otterbank Farami with chocolate mousse, Chantilly cream and vanilla shortbread

5. Hilden Brown Ale with Coolea Gouda-style cheese, fennel seed crackers and beer pickles

Matching Cider and Food

You might be surprised by how many foods can be paired with cider. Its natural fruitiness makes it easy to drink and easy to pair with food, plus its low ABV keeps things nice and light, making it a good choice for a midweek meal or those times when you want to relax with a glass of something but need to stay sharp to get through the rest of the week.

Dry ciders and sweet ciders are not created equal when it comes to matching cider and food, so take note of which kind you have at home or which you prefer and go from there. 'For food and cider matching, classic cider, made from classic cider apples such as Dabinett or Michelin in Ireland, has all the elements of a red wine: body, tannin and acidity, but obviously much less alcohol. Therefore with food you'd look for something in opposition to balance these elements – a protein, so meat and cheese,' advises Emma Tyrrell from Cider Ireland. 'That said, cider is a milder flavour, so you wouldn't necessarily look for anything as strong as game or lamb, but rather pork or chicken, or for cheese, a Brie or Camembert. Sweeter cider would work well with food with freshness and acidity, with hard and tangier cheeses or milder blue cheese.'

The same guidelines that apply to matching beer and food apply to cider too: decide whether you want to complement or contrast flavours, pair like with like and think seasonally.

- A good rule of thumb to start with is that if a certain dish or food goes well with white wine, then the chances are that it will also pair nicely with a fruity cider. This is because cider's lighter, more delicate flavour complements lighter, delicate foods.
- Pairing a fruity cider with fruity dishes is the easiest, most intuitive match. This applies to both sweet and savoury dishes – an apple crumble or pork with roasted apples will get a lift when served with an equally fruity cider.
- Cider loves pork. Pork belly, sausages, chops, ham and bacon will sing when served with a good cider to drink alongside, as the sweetness of the cider is a classic contrast to the salty pork.
- The delicate flavour of cider also plays well with chicken, as opposed to more heavy-hitting meats like beef, which would overwhelm it. Try hearty, wintry dishes like chicken casseroles, creamy chicken pot pies or a roast chicken with its crisp, salty skin with a cider. On the lighter side, try a chicken Caesar salad.
- Seafood and cider can work well together too. Light fish, oily fish and even oysters are a good match with dry cider, in much the same way that white wine and seafood is.

- Believe it or not, sweet cider matches well with Asian food and spicy curry, helping to cut through the heat. A dry cider, however, can unpleasantly enhance spiciness or acidity, so steer clear of those.
- When it comes to vegetables, think seasonally. Cider and, say, a butternut squash gratin, a creamy cauliflower cheese or a wild mushroom risotto will work well together. A sweet cider will also complement the sweetness of roasted autumnal vegetables – think roasted onions and fennel.
- Cider is also a beautiful match with cheese. Cider and a strong Cheddar is the most well-known match, but it also works well with Camembert and creamy cheeses. Sweet cider can also contrast nicely with salty blue cheeses, or try a dry cider with sheep's milk or goat's milk cheeses. The earthy mustiness of washed rind cheeses complements those same qualities in sweet cider. (See Chapter 7 for more.)

Pubs and Grub

There is perhaps no more beloved institution than the Irish pub, and yet for craft beer lovers it can seem like a case of water, water everywhere and not a drop to drink, with almost every pub in the country serving the same bland mass-market beers. All too often you walk into a restaurant that prides itself on using local, seasonal produce and name-checks its suppliers and food producers on the menu, only to turn to the drinks list and find nothing but big brands and imports. Where is the locally brewed Irish craft beer and cider to complement the local Irish food?

Things are looking up. In 2010 there were twenty-seven pubs selling craft beer in Ireland. Fast forward a few years and there are now over 500. And gastropubs, which were a late-twentieth-century invention as UK pubs sought to reinvent themselves by serving good food in addition to beer, have now spread to Ireland too.

Here are some of the best pubs for a craft pint, as well as the best gastropubs and restaurants that respect craft beer around the country – and that includes Michelin-starred restaurants. If you want to read more in-depth reviews of many of these places, check out the excellent *McKennas' Guides* (www.guides.ie) and Georgina Campbell's *Ireland Guide* (www.ireland-guide.com), both of which are invaluable, informative and trusted resources. Look up the directories on the Beoir website (www.beoir.org) for even more listings, and be sure to download the free BeoirFinder app to help you find nearby stockists of craft beer, no matter where you are in Ireland.

And remember, if your favourite pub or restaurant doesn't serve Irish craft beer or cider, ask them to!

> *'No, sir: There is nothing which has yet been contrived by man by which so much happiness is produced as by a good tavern or inn.'*
> *– Samuel Johnson*

Top 50 Pubs for a Craft Pint

57 The Headline, Dublin 8
Abbot's Ale House, Cork City
Against the Grain, Dublin 2
Alfie Byrne's, Dublin 2
Anchor Bar, Newcastle, Co. Down
Beerhouse, Dublin 1
Bernard Shaw, Dublin 2
Bierhaus, Cork City
Bittle's Bar, Belfast City
Black Sheep, Dublin 1
Brew Dock, Dublin 1
Brewery Corner, Kilkenny City
Cassidy's Bar, Dublin 2
Cotton Ball, Cork City
Crafty Fox, Limerick City
Cronin's, Crosshaven, Co. Cork
Darkey Kelly's, Dublin 1
Dicey Reilly's, Ballyshannon,
    Co. Donegal
Farrington's, Dublin 2
Fitzpatrick's Bar, Doolin, Co. Clare
Franciscan Well, Cork City
Furey's Pub, Sligo Town
Glen Tavern, Limerick City
Hanly's Bar, Strokestown,
    Co. Roscommon
Holland's of Bray, Co. Wicklow
J.W. Sweetman, Dublin 1
J.J. Harlow's, Roscommon Town
John Boyle Public House,
    Kildare Town

Kiwi's Bar, Portrush, Co. Antrim
L. Mulligan Grocer, Dublin 7
Logues, Letterkenny, Co. Donegal
Maguire's, Athlone,
    Co. Westmeath
McDaid's, Dublin 2
Mickey Finn's Pub, Redcross,
    Co. Wicklow
Nancy's of Ardara, Co. Donegal
O'Neill's of Suffolk Street,
    Dublin 2
Oslo Bar, Salthill, Co. Galway
P. Macs, Dublin 2
Phil Grimes Pub, Waterford City
Porterhouse, Dublin 2, Bray, Co.
    Wicklow and Cork City
Roadside Tavern, Lisdoonvarna,
    Co. Clare
Salthouse Bar, Galway City
Sheary's Bar and Lounge,
    Dublin 12
Simon Lambert and Sons,
    Wexford Town
Sky and the Ground,
    Wexford Town
Swagman Bar, Sligo Town
The Central, Navan, Co. Meath
The Dark Horse, Blackrock,
    Co. Dublin
The Folkhouse, Kinsale, Co. Cork
Wm Cairnes, Drogheda, Co. Louth

Top Gastropubs

Ashtons Gastropub, Dublin 14
Bar One, Castlebar, Co. Mayo
Blair's Inn, Blarney, Co. Cork
Brewer's House, Donaghmore,
    Co. Tyrone
Brook Inn, Glanmire, Co. Cork
Bull and Castle, Dublin 8
Chop House, Dublin 4
Clancy's Bar and Restaurant,
    Youghal, Co. Cork

Cottage Bar, Galway City
Crown Liquor Saloon, Belfast City
Derg Inn, Terryglass,
    Co. Tipperary
Dew Drop Inn, Kill, Co. Kildare
Dirty Duck Ale House, Holywood,
    Co. Down
EAT@Massimo, Galway City
Ely Gastro Bar, Dublin 2
Exchequer, Dublin 2

Fitzgerald's of Sandycove,
    Co. Dublin
Hargadon's, Sligo Town
Harte's Bar and Grill, Kildare Town
John Hewitt, Belfast City
L. Mulligan Grocer, Dublin 7
Larkin's Bar and Restaurant,
    Nenagh, Co. Tipperary
Lock 13, Sallins, Co. Kildare
Locke Bar and Oyster House,
    Limerick City
Mad Monk, Midleton, Co. Cork
McHugh's, Belfast City
Merry's Gastropub, Dungarvan,
    Co. Waterford
O'Dowd's, Roundstone,
    Co. Galway
Oarsman, Carrick-on-Shannon,
    Co. Leitrim

Parson's Nose, Hillsborough,
    Co. Down
Purty Kitchen, Monkstown,
    Co. Dublin
Scholar's Rest, Galway City
Taphouse, Dublin 6
The Reg, Waterford City
The Strand, New Ross,
    Co. Wexford
The Waterloo Bar and Grill,
    Dublin 4
Wallace Riverside Pub and
    Eatery, Lisburn, Co. Antrim
West Bar, Westport, Co. Mayo
White Horse Inn, Saintfield,
    Co. Down

Restaurants That Respect Craft Beer and Cider

An Canteen, Dingle, Co. Kerry
Aniar, Galway City
Barking Dog, Belfast City
Bodéga, Waterford City
Castle Restaurant, Cork City
Chapter One, Dublin 1
Cleaver East, Dublin 2
Cliff House Hotel, Ardmore,
    Co. Waterford
Dela, Galway City
Eastern Seaboard Bar and Grill,
    Drogheda, Co. Louth
Electric, Cork City
Fade Street Social, Dublin 2
Fatted Calf, Glasson,
    Co. Westmeath
Fenn's Quay, Cork City

Gastro Bar and Grill, Carlow Town
Grapevine, Kilkenny City
Harrys Bar and Restaurant,
    Bridgend, Co. Donegal
McCambridge's, Galway City
Molly's Yard, Belfast City
Mulberry Garden, Dublin 4
Ox, Belfast City
Sage Restaurant, Midleton,
    Co. Cork
Salty Dog Bistro, Bangor, Co. Down
Tap Room Restaurant, Lisburn,
    Co. Antrim
Whitefriar Grill, Dublin 2
Winding Stair, Dublin 1
Zuni, Kilkenny City

CHAPTER 7

MATCHING BEER AND CIDER WITH CHEESE

The Beara Peninsula in West Cork was the birthplace of the Irish farmhouse cheese-making renaissance in the 1970s. 'I'd be brushing the floor in the kitchen at night when the children were in bed, daydreaming about how we could have a great farmhouse cheese industry in Ireland, and sure enough, that came to pass,' says Veronica Steele. From Veronica's experiments in her kitchen came the iconic Milleens, a semi-soft washed rind cheese with an orange rind. In 1978 she started selling it to people like Ballymaloe's Myrtle Allen and Declan Ryan of the Michelin-starred Arbutus Lodge, who wanted to stock it in their restaurants. The demand wasn't just from people who wanted to eat the cheese; it also came from those who wanted to learn how to make it for themselves.

Before Milleens, the only cheese that was widely available in Ireland was Cheddar, a traditional British cheese style that was made on a commercial scale, but Veronica was now demonstrating how a semi-soft cheese could be made with only a small amount of milk. She may have been just one woman standing in a kitchen in West Cork dreaming up a cheese industry, but by passing on that knowledge to others – notably Giana Ferguson of Gubbeen and Durrus's Jeffa Gill – she single-handedly played a large part in the revival of Irish farmhouse cheese-making.

From humble beginnings in the 1970s to a thriving farmhouse cheese industry in the 2010s, there are now more than sixty registered producers in the country, making about 1,100 tons of farmhouse cheese, €4.5 million worth of which is exported.

Cheese and Beer: A Match Made in Heaven

Even though wine has traditionally been served with cheese, it is actually very difficult to match them. The idea that they go together is surely one of the biggest myths in the food world. Wine writers had the field to themselves for years and consistently put forward the idea that wine and cheese were made for each other, but there is a growing recognition that cheese actually goes together better with good beer or cider.

Brewers and cheese-makers start with a few simple ingredients: barley, hops, yeast and water for beer; milk, a starter culture, rennet and salt for cheese. Each producer takes the basics and transforms them into something that reflects both the character of the maker and a sense of place. In both industries, innovation and creativity are balanced with tradition. As you sample a selection of Irish cheese, you taste the unique character of each cheese-maker; match that with a local craft beer or cider and you get a real sense of *terroir*, Irish style. This is also the easiest way to pair them. Pick a local farmhouse cheese, put it together with a beer made just up the road – often using the same water – or a local cider and try a little experimental matching for yourself.

In 2013, Knockdrinna's Helen Finnegan created a new washed rind cheese called Brewer's Gold using organic milk from The Little Milk Company and a selection of ales from Carlow Brewing, Dungarvan Brewing and Eight Degrees Brewing. This semi-soft golden cheese has a gloriously complex flavour that is best accompanied with simple oatcakes and a fruity red ale or a dark, slightly bitter porter.

Top Tips for Pairing Cheese and Beer

1. **Contrast:** Put completely different elements together and enjoy the contrast. Taste the aromatic hops of a pale ale alongside the bite of an intense blue cheese to bring out another level of complexity in both.
2. **Complement:** Matching harmonising flavours lets them both shine. Take that same blue cheese and match it with a porter to enhance the beer's malty, rich sweetness.
3. **Cut:** The bitterness of hops cuts straight through the palate-coating richness of cheese. Carbonation also has an important role to play here: the bubbles scrub your tongue with each sip, allowing you to really taste what you are eating.
4. **Colour:** In general, lighter-coloured beers go with fresher, more delicate cheeses, while dark, intense brews work better with a similarly intensely flavoured cheese. That said, sometimes beers don't always look the way they taste – watch out for black IPAs!
5. **Balance:** Be careful not to overpower either component. A soft, mild goat's cheese could easily be overwhelmed by a strong ale.

Cold is the real enemy here. If either the cheese or beer has been in the fridge too long, then you won't get their full flavour. Remove cheese from the fridge at least half an hour before you intend to eat it, and between 5°C and 11°C is a good serving temperature for most craft beers. Check individual labels for more information.

Cheese and Cider

Cider and cheese are natural companions. Hard cheese and cider are a traditional English pairing, but there are a lot more options to play with than just Cheddar. Carbonation cuts through creamy, rich cheese, while the acidity of the apples enhances its complexity. Medium-dry ciders go well with Camembert-style cheese like Cooleeney or Wicklow Baun, or young, buttery Cheddars such as Bay Lough and Coolattin. The more tannic ciders are also a good match with something with a bit more bite, like an aged Cratloe Hills sheep milk cheese or Milleens. Have a sweeter cider on hand? Go blue – it makes for an irresistibly delicious salty–sweet combination. That said, the combination of Mac Ivors Traditional Dry with the raw milk Bellingham Blue got a lot of people's attention at the 2013 Irish Craft Beer and Cider Festival.

Matching Cheese with Beer and Cider

Mild, fresh

These are soft, milky cheeses that have not been ripened or aged. They have no rind, a delicate flavour and are meant to be eaten while still very young. This is a diverse category that includes fresh goat's cheese, such as Bluebell Falls Cygnus, the feta-style Knockalara Waterford Greek Cheese and Toonsbridge Buffalo Mozzarella.

Match: Avoid overpowering such delicate flavours by going for something crisp, fresh and subtle. Try a lager or pilsner, such as 5 Lamps Dublin Lager, or a light wheat beer like White Gypsy's Blond weissbier. A blonde ale – try Hilden's Belfast Blonde – will also let these cheeses shine.

Semi-soft, white rind

Made in the style of Camembert and Brie, these buttery, rich cheeses have a white bloomy rind that ripens from the outside in. Irish examples include Cooleeney, St Killian and Wicklow Baun.

Match: The buttery texture of this cheese needs to be cut with a pale ale or blonde ale like McGrath's Irish Blonde Ale #5, Kinsale Pale Ale or Dungarvan Brewing's Helvick Gold. Or take a tip from Normandy and pair cider with this style – the sweet tartness of the medium-dry Stonewell Cider will enhance the savoury cheese.

Semi-soft, washed rind

Aromatic, earthy and often intensely pungent. Some of Ireland's best-known cheeses, including Durrus, Gubbeen and Milleens, are in this category, as is Brewer's Gold.

Match: Notoriously difficult to match with wine, washed rind cheese and beer are a killer combination. With the younger cheeses, try a malty, fruity red like Dungarvan Brewing's Copper Coast or Brú Brewery's Rua. White Gypsy has a dubbel that would stand up against the more extreme examples, or change tack and try a dry cider, like Double L Bone Dry Cider.

Alpine

In the style of Comté, Gruyère or Beaufort, these large, hard cheeses have a delicious smooth texture and nutty flavour. St Gall is sold while still young, but other examples, such as Hibernia, are aged for a minimum of twelve months.

Match: Ideally paired with a saison, lambic or the Brown Paper Bag Project's salty, sour Gøse, but steer clear of the citrus and pine flavours in ultra-hoppy beers, which can be overwhelming. Hilden Number Four and Bo Bristle's American Brown Ale have a malt-driven sweetness that will enhance the cheese's caramel characteristics, while a malty stout or porter can complement these subtly sweet cheeses.

Hard

Hard Gouda and Cheddar-style cheeses have a dense texture that dries out and becomes crumbly with age. The full flavours of Mossfield, Hegarty's Cheddar, Mount Callan Cheddar or a mature Coolea make them stars in the kitchen as well as on the cheeseboard.

Match: An IPA like Galway Hooker brings a note of bitterness that works well with a younger hard cheese, while O'Hara's Double IPA has enough hops to stand against something with more intense flavours. A brown ale will harmonise nicely with an aged cheese like mature Coolea, which has similar nutty notes. If you have a particularly sharp Cheddar, go for a savoury–sweet pairing with a crisp Longueville House Cider.

Blue

With distinctively strong, pungent flavours, blue cheese can dominate proceedings – taste the power of an aged Cashel Blue or Bellingham Blue – or it can be delicate and versatile, like Wicklow Blue.

Match: This can make for a showstopping end to a food-matching meal with beer or cider. A strong blue cheese can stand up against a weighty beer like an imperial stout from White Gypsy or Porterhouse. The more delicate blues will work beautifully with the Dark Arts Porter from Trouble Brewing. Alternatively, a hoppy IPA or a dry cider will cut the richness and complement the mouldy tang.

Goat

Ranging widely in texture, from the cottage cheese-style Cléire to hard and crumbly like Corleggy and Orion, these all share a similarly piquant, dry flavour from the goat milk used.

Match: Match dry cider from Tempted? with young, fresh cheeses, or try a tart, light-bodied wheat beer like the Franciscan Well's Friar Weisse. Sticking with cider, pick something tannic, such as Mac Ivor's Traditional Dry, for the aged, hard cheeses.

How to Host a Beer, Cider and Cheese-Tasting Evening

Send out invitations to a beer, cider and cheese-tasting evening and you are going to get attention immediately. This is easy entertaining at its best: casual, fun and guaranteed to have everyone talking to each other.

Per person you'll need:

- A plate for cheese
- Two or three small shot glasses
- A glass of water
- A selection of palate-cleaning nibbles like crusty bread, pretzels, breadsticks, nuts and fresh and dried fruit
- A notebook or handouts to record your favourite combinations (you might not remember them in the morning!)

Beer, Cider and Cheese Matching Cheat Sheet

Cheese	Examples	Beer/Cider
Mild, fresh	Bluebell Falls Cygnus Knockalara Greek Cheese Toonsbridge Buffalo Mozzarella	Blonde ale Lager Pilsner Wheat beer
Semi-soft, white rind	Cooleeney St Killian Wicklow Baun	Blonde ale Pale ale Medium-dry cider
Semi-soft, washed rind	Brewer's Gold Durrus Gubbeen Milleens	Dubbel Red ale
Alpine	Hibernia St Gall	Brown ale Lambic Saison Stout
Hard	Coolea Hegarty's Cheddar Mossfield Mount Callan Cheddar	Brown ale IPA Stout Cider
Blue	Bellingham Blue Cashel Blue Crozier Blue Wicklow Blue	IPA Stout Dry cider
Goat	Cléire Corleggy Orion	Wheat beer Dry cider

The cheese

When you are assembling a cheeseboard at home, go for a small selection and get decent-sized pieces of each cheese. Think along the lines of a chunk of Wilma's Killorglin, a whole mini Ardrahan and a hunk of Crozier Blue. Offer a contrast: a hard cheese, a semi-soft and a blue makes for a good range of flavour and texture. The staff in a good cheese shop or market stall can tell you what is in prime condition. Another alternative is to serve a cheese for sharing, like the baked Irish Brie with red ale caramel on page 184.

> We asked Elisabeth Ryan from Sheridans Cheesemongers which Irish farmhouse cheeses she would put together on a board, and she gave us three different board suggestions. These are not hard and fast guidelines – at the end of the day, you should choose the cheeses you like best.
>
> - **The Crowd Pleaser:** Gubbeen, Hegarty's Cheddar and Cooleeney
> - **The Subtle Board:** Triskel or St Tola, Ardrahan and Durrus
> - **The Strong Board:** Coolea, Milleens and Bellingham Blue

The drinks

Go for five or six different beers and ciders so that you can try plenty of different permutations and combinations. Ask your local off-licence for suggestions that cover a range of styles. Depending on the size of your tasting glasses, you should be able to get three or four tastings per 330ml bottle or five or six tastings per 500ml bottle.

Start tasting!

Get guests to cut a piece of each cheese, pour some drinks and work away. Discuss. Argue. Laugh. Come away feeling like you have some new favourites.

Sheridans Cheesemongers: A National Treasure

In 1995 Kevin and Seamus Sheridan started selling cheese at a market in Galway, and they haven't stopped since. Sheridans Cheesemongers now has shops in Galway, Dublin and an outlet in Waterford's Ardkeen Quality Food Store, along with weekly markets and an annual food festival at their headquarters at Virginia Road Station, Co. Meath. What the Sheridan brothers don't know about cheese and Irish food producers isn't worth knowing.

'At Sheridans we have been having fun matching beers and cheeses for many years,' says Kevin. 'It has always made sense to us that our great Irish cheeses would work well with Irish beers, coming as they do from the same soil and climate as well as culture. It has been a huge pleasure for us to watch the extraordinary growth of craft brewing in Ireland over the past ten years or so. It is now the case that together, farmhouse cheeses and craft beers are the two most successful artisan food sectors, and it is wonderful how they complement each other so well. As we always say when trying wine, beers or any accompaniments with cheese, there are no set rules. Don't let preconceptions get in your way; enjoy trying your own combinations. Here are a few of our favourites.'

1. Dungarvan Brewing Black Rock Stout and Cashel Blue

It just works so well, it is almost a cliché already! The chocolatey rich tones of stout roll over the sweet and salty creaminess of Cashel perfectly. Both are improved by the pairing, which is what we are always after. Cashel is a relatively mild blue, but has a lovely sweetness that brings out the sweeter side of the stout. Bellingham Blue and Crozier Blue are also great with a good stout.

2. Eight Degrees Brewing Howling Gale Ale and Coolea Mature

Our mature Coolea made only with summer milk is aged for around two years, allowing all the flavours to come together and intensify, and is a cheese that works well with almost any beer. It is so robust it can stand up to a big stout, but the Howling Gale has a freshness that cuts across the big caramel flavours of the Coolea and brings out the best in this great cheese.

3. O'Hara's Curim Gold Wheat Beer and Killeen Goat's Cheese

This fruity and fresh-tasting beer really works alongside this quite subtle goat's cheese. Made in Galway by Marion Roeleveld using milk from her own goat herd, this is one of our most popular cheeses. The sweet finish of the beer brings out the sweet, milky flavours in the cheese, and the delicate floral aroma of Killeen mingles well with the fruity nose of the beer.

4. Porterhouse Hersbrucker Pilsner and Knockanore Smoked

Another great match is smoked cheese and light beers or lager. Eamonn Lonergan smokes his Knockanore cheese after he has aged it for six months using a traditional cold smoke, allowing the cheese to take on a deep, rich, smoky flavour. This pilsner has a nice sharpness that complements the heavy smokiness of the cheese, and the soft hops and malt blend into the rich Cheddar flavour.

5. Stonewell Dry Cider and Durrus

Dry cider is a great accompaniment to many foods, including cheeses. We love it with Irish washed rind cheese such as Durrus. Made on the Sheep's Head peninsula, West Cork, Durrus is a delicate yet earthy cheese. Some beers can bring out a bitterness in this type of cheese, but dry cider emphasises its sweetness, and the crispness of this cider contrasts beautifully with the mild pungency of the cheese.

Part three

COOK

CHAPTER 8

COOKING WITH CRAFT BEER AND CIDER

Cooking with Craft Beer

We're no strangers to cooking with wine – think of classics like *boeuf bourguignon*, *coq au vin*, mussels steamed in white wine or adding a splash of red to your Bolognese sauce. There is also a long tradition of cooking with beer. This is particularly true in Belgium, where they even have a name for it, *cuisine à la bière*, and where they take their beer so seriously that they have even applied to UNESCO to have their beer culture officially protected and recognised. And of course Ireland has its fair share of dishes made with a certain stout.

It doesn't always have to just be about one big brand. Celebrate the flavour of craft beers by using them in your cooking, taking advantage of their hop bitterness, sweet malts and yeasty complexity.

Hops

Hops bring a refreshing bitterness to a dish, but it is easy to go too far. If you deglaze a pan with a hoppy IPA or use it in a stew that will simmer away for a couple of hours, you *will* regret it. The bitterness increases as the liquid reduces, and depending on the beer, it can make your dish almost inedible. If this happens, try rebalancing the flavours with some sweetness – tomato ketchup, brown sugar or even balsamic vinegar can rescue it. Treat a highly hopped beer as you would lemon juice: useful for adding a spritz of flavour to counteract richness without overloading the dish.

Malt

Sweet malts complement similarly sweet flavours, which is why darker beers (porters, stouts or bock lagers) go so well in beef stews, chillies or shepherd's pies that include caramelised onions and sweet root vegetables like carrots. If you are using beer as a cooking liquid or for gravy, don't overdo it. You want people to say 'what was that flavour?' rather than 'what was *in* that stew?' Check your liquid measurements and don't use beer for more than half the total amount.

Yeast

Beer in breads and batters for things like waffles, pancakes and fritters works brilliantly. It showcases the beer's fermented flavours and complements the yeasty flavours in your baking, especially with bottle-conditioned or wheat beers. Beer also acts as a leavening agent, making batters lighter and bread rise faster, so in the case of yeast baking you may need to reduce the amount of yeast used.

Five Easy Ways to Cook with Craft Beer

You always hear that you should cook with a wine you would be happy to drink, and the same goes for cooking with beer. The depth of flavour you find in a craft beer goes right into the pot or mixing bowl, adding complexity to the food. Here are five easy ideas for using beer in your cooking:

- Pour a cup of red ale over a chicken before you roast it.
- Poach some fat butcher sausages in porter before they hit the barbecue.
- Add a couple of tablespoons of stout to a mushroom soup.
- Make a salted caramel ale sauce to serve over ice cream.
- Try one of the flavoured beers in waffles, such as Kinnegar's Yannaroddy coconut porter or the seasonal pumpkin ale from Trouble Brewing.

The easiest way to measure the beer is to use a digital scale and weigh it, or else allow it to go flat before you try to pour it into your measuring cups.

When you are cooking with beer, you don't necessarily need to match the finished dish with the same beer. Try contrasting flavours – for example, pour a snappy pilsner to go with the porter burgers on page 166.

Worried about the level of alcohol in the finished dish? Anywhere from 15% to 95% of it burns off, depending on how long you cook it for. If you only add it to boiling liquid and remove it from the heat, it will still pack a boozy punch. If you simmer it for 2.5 hours, only 5% of the alcohol will be left.

Top Tips for Cooking with Cider

The pure fermented appley lusciousness of good cider makes it an especially versatile ingredient. There is a lot to play with here: fruity sweetness and refreshing acidity, a whole orchard-worth of apple flavours and a lovely depth from the fermentation.

- **It makes a great sauce:** Try slow-roasting a shoulder of pork on a bed of onions and cider, skimming off the fat and reducing the liquid to make an intense jus to accompany the meat.
- **Use it for steaming:** Take a pot of mussels, steam them open with a glass of cider and finish off the juices with a dash of cream (see Donal Skehan's recipe on page 172). It is also good for poaching white fish fillets or even pears.
- **It gives great flavour to a cake:** In the autumn, add cider to a cake that also includes plenty of apples, some crunchy nuts and warm spices like cinnamon and cardamom.
- **Gently braise with cider:** Braise chicken, lamb or rabbit in cider for a simple and warming one-pot meal. Try pairing meat and cider from nearby producers for a real local match.
- **Just use pig:** Any dish involving something piggy plus cider is going to be a classic. For a cheap and cheerful supper, fry up some crisp eating apples and black pudding, pour over a little cider, simmer and serve on creamy mashed potatoes, accompanied with a glass of the cider.

We have gathered together recipes showcasing craft beer and cider from artisan food producers, restaurant owners and chefs, food writers and bloggers from around Ireland as well as a few of our own. If you thought that beer was only good for a beef and stout stew or that cider was only to be used in Normandy pork, you are going to be pleasantly surprised.

Beef, Chorizo and Ale Stew
Serves 6–8

A warming bowl of stew, a chunky soup or chowder or a golden, steaming pot pie all beg for a beer to be served alongside them. But beer is also fantastic when added directly to the dish itself. Beers like porters, stouts and ales lend themselves particularly well to hearty dishes, such as stew. For something lighter, like a seafood chowder, try adding a splash of pilsner in place of the usual white wine. An ale with plenty of flavour is needed to hold its own against the beef and chorizo here – try Eight Degrees Howling Gale Ale or Galway Hooker. As with any stew, this tastes even better the day after you make it, so you might consider cooking it a day in advance.

1kg stewing beef (such as shin or cheek), cut into bite-sized pieces
salt and freshly ground black pepper
2 tablespoons plain flour
rapeseed or olive oil
200–300g dry-cured Spanish chorizo, cut into bite-sized pieces
3 red onions, roughly chopped
3 carrots, peeled and roughly chopped
2 celery stalks, thickly sliced
3 garlic cloves, minced
1 tablespoon chopped fresh thyme leaves (or 1 teaspoon dried thyme)
1 tablespoon tomato purée
500ml pale ale
500ml beef or chicken stock
chopped fresh parsley, to garnish
mashed potatoes or crusty bread, to serve

Preheat the oven to 130°C.

Put the beef in a large bowl and sprinkle over 1 teaspoon of salt and plenty of freshly ground black pepper. Add the flour and toss the beef in it until it all has a light dusting. Heat some rapeseed or olive oil in a large ovenproof casserole (or a large pot that you can leave to simmer on the stovetop if you don't have an ovenproof one) and brown the beef in batches over a medium-high heat, making sure not to crowd the pot or the meat won't brown properly. Add more oil in between batches if the pot looks too dry. Remove the beef from the pot and set aside.

Add in the chorizo and cook for a few minutes, until it has started to release its oils, then add the onions, carrots and celery and cook, covered, for about 10 minutes, until the vegetables have softened but not browned.

Add the garlic and thyme and cook for 1 minute, then add the tomato purée and cook for 1 minute more. Pour in the ale, scraping up any browned bits that have stuck to the bottom of the pot.

Return the beef to the pot and top up with enough stock to cover the beef fully (add all the stock if you like a thinner stew; add less if you like a more concentrated broth). Bring up to a lively simmer, then cover and put in the oven for 3–4 hours (or simmer on the stovetop on a low heat with the lid on), stirring a few times. The stew is ready when the beef easily falls apart when you prod it with a fork. Garnish with lots of chopped fresh parsley and serve with mashed potatoes or crusty bread.

Leek, Chicken and Ale Stew
Serves 6

When it's not beer in our dinners, it's barley – and sometimes both. Food writer Lilly Higgins first published this recipe in her Sunday Business Post *column, showing a mainstream audience how cooking with beer is moving beyond beef and stout stew. She used a red ale, as the caramel notes from the ale complement the sweet leeks and caramelised flavours of leftover roast chicken. Try something like Bo Bristle's amber ale, Brú Rua or McGrath's Irish Red #1. We have also made it with a mild blonde ale, such as Donegal Brewing's Donegal Blonde or even Independent Brewing's Gold Ale. Just be careful not to overwhelm the delicate flavours with too much hops.*

2 tablespoons butter
2 leeks, finely sliced
1 teaspoon Dijon mustard
330ml red ale or blonde ale
300g pearl barley
900ml chicken stock

300g cooked chicken (or 3 small chicken fillets, poached), roughly chopped
sea salt and freshly ground black pepper

Melt the butter in a large heavy-based pan on a medium heat with a few tablespoons of water, then sauté the leeks for a few minutes with the lid on. Stir in the mustard, then pour in the ale. Add in the barley and simmer for a minute or so before pouring over the stock and adding the chicken. Bring to the boil, then lower the heat to a simmer and cover with the lid again.

Leave it to bubble away gently for 15–20 minutes, until the barley is only just cooked. Taste for seasoning, adding plenty of sea salt and freshly ground black pepper. Ladle into bowls and serve with kale, broccoli or carrots, or just eat a big steaming bowl of it, unadorned, for some rib-sticking comfort food.

Beef, Beer and Blue Cheese Pot Pies

Serves 4–6

There is nothing wrong with a classic beef and stout stew, but what if you upped the ante on the stout and added some blue cheese too? And what if you capped it with a flaky puff pastry lid and called it a pot pie instead? Now you're talking.

1kg stewing beef (such as shin or cheek), cut into bite-sized pieces
salt and freshly ground black pepper
3 tablespoons plain flour
rapeseed or olive oil
2 red onions, chopped
2 carrots, peeled and chopped
3 garlic cloves, chopped
1 teaspoon chopped fresh thyme leaves (or ½ teaspoon dried thyme)
500ml stout
125g crumbled blue cheese
1 sheet of ready-rolled puff pastry
1 egg, beaten

Preheat the oven to 130°C.

Put the beef in a large bowl and sprinkle over 1 teaspoon of salt and plenty of freshly ground black pepper. Add the flour and toss the beef in it until it all has a light dusting. Heat some rapeseed or olive oil in a large ovenproof casserole and brown the beef in batches over a medium-high heat, making sure not to crowd the pot or the meat won't brown properly. Add more oil in between batches if needed. Remove the beef from the pot and set aside.

Add another splash of oil to the pot, then add the onions and carrots along with a pinch of salt so that the onions don't brown. Cover the pot and cook for 10–15 minutes, stirring occasionally, until the vegetables are soft but not browned. Add the garlic, thyme and a generous seasoning of salt and pepper and cook for 1 or 2 minutes more.

Pour in the stout, scraping up any browned bits that have stuck to the bottom of the pot. Return the beef to the pot and bring up to a lively simmer, then cover and put in the oven for 3–4 hours (or simmer on the stovetop on a low heat with the lid on), stirring a few times. You will know it's done when the beef easily falls apart when you prod it with a fork and the stout has reduced right down – it's a pot pie filling, not a stew, so you want it to be nice and thick. Stir in the cheese, then taste it and adjust the seasoning if necessary.

Raise the oven temperature to 190°C. Place one large ovenproof pie dish or individual dishes or ramekins onto a baking tray just in case any filling bubbles up and over the sides, then spoon the stew into the dish(es). Roll out the pastry a little on a lightly floured countertop, then cut to fit the top of the dish. Rub the edges of the dish with a little water or some of the beaten egg to help the pastry stick in place, then place the pastry lid on top. Brush the pastry with the beaten egg (not too much or the pastry won't rise properly), then cook in the oven for 20–30 minutes, until the pastry has risen and is golden. Allow to stand for 10 minutes before digging in.

Porter Burgers
Makes 6 burgers

This recipe comes from The Irish Beef Book *(Gill & Macmillan), written by fifth-generation Tipperary butcher Pat Whelan and food writer Katy McGuinness, which celebrates the butcher's craft. It's the kind of book that every self-respecting kitchen needs to have a copy of – equal parts timeless resource book and irresistible recipes. The porter (or you could use a stout) gives these burgers real depth of flavour. They are great as they are and unadorned, but they are spectacular with a few thick slices of blue cheese on top, such as Cashel Blue or Bellingham Blue.*

1 tablespoon rapeseed oil
1 large onion, finely chopped
1 kg coarsely ground beef mince
    (80:20 ratio of meat to fat)
100ml porter or stout
2 tablespoons brown
    breadcrumbs

2 teaspoons finely chopped
    parsley and/or thyme
1 teaspoon sea salt
freshly ground black pepper

Heat the oil in a frying pan over a low heat and slowly fry the onion for about 20 minutes, until soft and slightly browned. Leave to cool.

Combine the beef with the onion, stout, breadcrumbs, herbs and seasoning. Divide the meat mixture into 6 portions and form into flat burgers, pressing a dimple into the centre of each, which will help them to remain flat during cooking.

Cover and chill for an hour so that the burgers will retain their shape and hold together during cooking.

Cook on the barbecue or on a heavy, cast iron ridged griddle pan preheated until it is smoking.

There is no need to oil either the grill or the burgers, but if you are concerned that they might stick (because you have used very lean meat), lightly brush the burgers with oil. Place on the grill for about 4 minutes per side for medium rare.

Irish Ale-Battered Fish with Chickpea Chips and Lemon Aioli
Serves 4–6

Imen McDonnell was working in television production in America when an Irish farmer on holidays unexpectedly swept her off her feet. She married him, and she now lives on his family farm in Co. Limerick and has made a name for herself in the Irish food scene. Imen writes the Farmette blog and a weekly column for Irish Country Living, *directed and produced the short film* Small Green Fields *about Irish food, and her first cookbook is due out in the autumn of 2015. We love her fresh twists on Irish classics, like this version of fish and chips, but with an Irish craft ale batter and chickpea chips instead of the usual potato. This makes a lot of chips, depending on how thinly you cut them, so you could probably get away with halving the recipe and still have plenty for four greedy adults. As for the beer, the more flavourful the ale is, the more flavourful the beer batter will be. Good ones to try are O'Hara's Irish Pale Ale or even Helvick Gold from Dungarvan Brewing.*

For the beer-battered fish:
225g self-raising flour
1 egg, lightly whisked
375ml chilled pale ale
salt and freshly ground black
    pepper
vegetable oil, to deep-fry
8 x 120g white fish fillets (such as
    cod or hake)
lemon wedges, to serve

For the chickpea chips:
425g gram flour (aka chickpea
    flour, available at natural food
    stores)
170g medium-ground maize meal
    (cornmeal), plus extra for
    dusting

2 garlic cloves, finely grated
2 tablespoons coarse salt
zest of 2 lemons
large handful of fresh parsley,
    finely chopped
1 tablespoon finely chopped
    fresh rosemary
vegetable oil, for frying

For the lemon aioli:
150g mayonnaise
1 garlic clove, minced
3 tablespoons lemon juice
½ teaspoon lemon zest
sea salt and freshly ground black
    pepper, to taste

First, make the chickpea chips. Combine the gram flour, maize meal, garlic, salt and 1.6 litres of cold water in a stainless steel pot over a high heat. Whisk gently to prevent it from sticking on the bottom, but don't over-whisk it or the final product will 'soufflé' and fall.

Once the mixture begins to thicken and bubble (after about 3–4 minutes), reduce the heat to medium and switch to a rubber spatula. Stir in the lemon zest, parsley and rosemary and continue stirring to prevent it from sticking. When the mixture pulls away from the sides of the pot and is becoming hard to stir (after about 6–8 minutes), transfer it to a rimmed Swiss roll tray lined with non-stick parchment paper and spread it out evenly. If it is too thick to spread with the spatula, let it cool just enough so that you can touch it, then run your hands under the tap and press it out evenly with your damp palms. Cover with a sheet of plastic wrap and top with another baking tray. Refrigerate for 4 hours, until completely cold and set.

Carefully remove the slab from the tray by gently lifting the bottom layer of parchment paper onto a cutting board. Remove the plastic wrap, then cut into chips about 8cm long.

Add a few centimetres worth of vegetable oil to a large saucepan. Heat the oil to 190°C over a high heat – when the oil is ready, a cube of bread dropped into it will turn golden brown in 10 seconds. Lower the heat to medium, toss the chips lightly in some extra maize meal and deep-fry them in small batches until crispy, about 2 minutes per side. Remove and drain on a plate lined with kitchen paper and keep warm.

To make the lemon aioli, simply mix all the ingredients together in a medium bowl.

To prepare the fish, place the flour in a bowl. Add the egg and stir to combine. Gradually whisk in the beer until the batter is smooth, then season with salt and pepper. Cover and place in the fridge for 30 minutes to rest.

Add enough vegetable oil to a large saucepan to reach a depth of about 4cm, or enough oil so that it reaches at least halfway up the sides of the fish fillets. Heat the oil to 190°C over a high heat – when the oil is ready, a cube of bread dropped into it will turn golden brown in 10 seconds. Dip 2 pieces of fish into the batter to coat them and quickly slide them into the hot oil before too much batter drips away. Deep-fry for 3–4 minutes on each side, until golden brown, crispy and cooked through. Don't be tempted to move the fish around in the pan during that time or the batter might slide off. Transfer to a plate lined with kitchen paper. Repeat in 3 more batches with the remaining fish and batter, reheating the oil between batches.

Serve the fish with the chickpea chips and the lemon aioli as a dipping sauce and lemon wedges on the side.

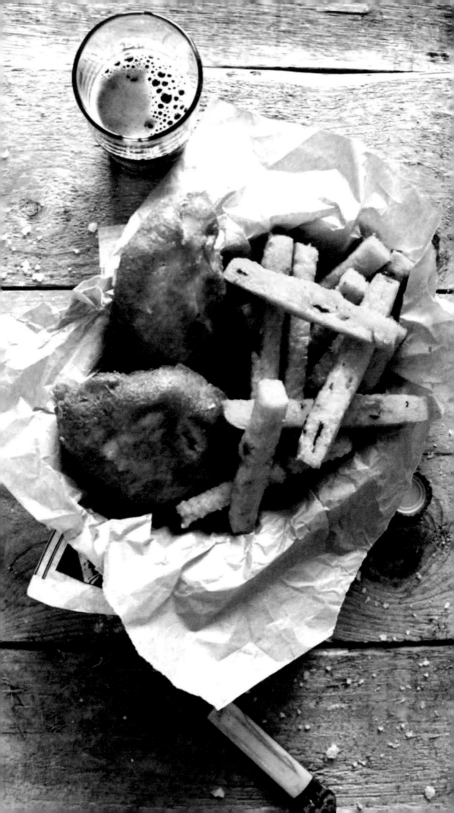

Cider-Brined Pork Fillet with Apples, Onions and Fennel

Serves 4–6

Brining meat is a fail-safe way to infuse it with flavour and to keep it from drying out when you cook it. We have brined pork tenderloin fillets in cider here for an appley flavour that really comes through, but thick-cut pork chops would work just as well too – preheat the grill instead of the oven and grill for about 5 minutes per side, until cooked through. To make this a one-tray dinner, parboil some baby potatoes for 5 minutes, cut them in half and add them to the roasting dish instead of mashed potatoes. One for your favourite autumn dinners repertoire.

1 litre medium or sweet cider
3 tablespoons coarse salt
2 x 500g pork tenderloin fillets
olive oil
salt and freshly ground black pepper

4 crisp red eating apples (such as Braeburn), peeled and cored
2 fennel bulbs, tops trimmed off
2 large onions
mashed potatoes, to serve

Place the cider and salt in a pot and heat until the salt has only just dissolved. Allow the brine to cool completely in the fridge (this step is very important – placing meat in a warm brine would start to cook it and would encourage unwanted bacterial growth). Place the pork in a large ziplock bag or a large casserole dish and pour the cooled brine over. Seal or cover tightly and refrigerate for at least 12 hours, but ideally overnight. Don't let the meat sit in the brine for more than 24 hours or it will be too salty.

The next day, preheat the oven to 225°C.

Heat a splash of olive oil in a large frying pan over a medium heat. Remove the pork from the brine and pat it dry with kitchen paper (throw away the brine at this point). Season with salt and pepper, but go easy on the salt since the pork will already be quite salty now from the brine. Sear the pork fillet all over until nicely browned, then set aside.

Cut the apples, fennel and onions into wedges that are all roughly the same size. Add to the pan and sauté for about 10 minutes, until they have a nice bit of colour and have started to soften. You may have to do this in batches.

Transfer the apples, fennel and onions to a large casserole dish or baking tray, then nestle the pork fillets on top. Roast in the oven for 15–25 minutes, until a thermometer inserted into the thickest part of the pork fillet reads 63°C (145°F). The cooking time will depend on how thick the fillet is, so start checking it after 15 minutes and give it more time if needed. The thickest part may still be a little pink when you cut into it, but that's okay as long as the temperature is 63°C (145°F).

Transfer the pork to a chopping board, loosely tent it with foil and allow to rest for 10 minutes, then carve into thick slices. Spoon the roasted apples, fennel and onions into a serving dish, arrange the pork alongside and serve with creamy mashed potatoes.

Mussels with Bacon and Irish Cider

Serves 4

TV cook and author Donal Skehan says that mussels have a reputation for being difficult, but this is just not true. In reality, the hardest part is washing them. Place them in cold water (they should close – if they don't, throw them away). Scrub any dirt off the surface of the mussels and remove the beard with a small knife. If you can get this down, you won't have any trouble. They take minutes to cook, so they are the perfect little starter. Serve the pot straight to the table from the stove and clunk large spoonfuls of the cooked, steaming mussels onto guests' plates. Make sure to serve with some chunky bread to mop up the juices.

200g pancetta pieces or diced
    bacon
knob of butter
1 medium onion, finely chopped
3 garlic cloves, crushed
400ml medium or sweet cider
1.5kg mussels, washed and
    beards removed

4 tablespoons cream
handful of chopped fresh parsley
sea salt and freshly ground black
    pepper
crusty bread, to serve

Discard any mussels that are open before cooking and any that stay closed after cooking.

Place a large pot over a high heat and brown the pancetta pieces until just golden and sizzling. Reduce the heat to medium, add in the knob of butter and allow it to melt. Add the chopped onion and cook gently for about 5 minutes, covered, until soft but not browned. Stir in the garlic and cook, uncovered, for 1 minute more.

Pour in the cider and allow it to bubble away for a few minutes so that all the flavours mingle together. Add in the mussels, cover the pot with a lid and allow them to steam for about 4 minutes, until they open. Give the pot a good shake once or twice during the cooking time.

Remove from the heat, stir in the cream and parsley and season with sea salt and ground black pepper. Serve with some crusty bread to mop up the salty, cidery liquid.

Beer and bread

Beer and bread are two sides of the same coin. The Germans even call their doppelbock 'liquid bread', and ale and bread were historically both important sources of nutrition. Ancient brewing began with the making of bread, and the words *brewing* and *bread* are even linguistically related.

So why not get the best of both worlds and use beer directly in bread? The next time you make bread – or even pizza dough – try replacing half of the liquid with beer. The malt in the beer will give it a slightly nutty flavour and it will give a good colour to the bread too. Just remember that the stronger the flavour of the beer, the stronger the flavour of the bread.

Barm

Barm is the yeasty froth that bubbles up on top of beer, wine or other malt liquors when it is fermenting. It was used to leaven bread or kick-start fermentation in a new batch of beer, much like a sourdough bread starter. In Old English, one of the meanings for the word *beorma* (from which the word *barm* is derived) was 'head of beer'.

In Ireland we are familiar with barm from barmbrack, the traditional Halloween bread that originally would have used barm before commercial yeast became widely available. The 'brack' part of barmbrack comes from the Irish word *breac*, meaning 'speckled' – barmbrack is dotted with dried fruit and candied peel.

In her book *Irish Traditional Cooking,* Darina Allen includes instructions for how to make barm from a recipe dated 26 August 1851: 'Take one ounce of hops with a plateful of malt and boil in two gallons of water for an hour and then strain them, when milk is warm add 2lbs of flour with a pint of old barm, jug it up well and set it in a warm place and it will be fit for use next day. 1 pint and about a wine glass will be sufficient for 4 quarts of flour.'

Dilisk and Stout Brown Soda Bread
Makes 1 x 900g loaf

2013 was the year of seaweed. We watched it pop up in salads, fish batters and at food festivals nationwide. The well-timed publication of Sally McKenna's fascinating and accessible Extreme Greens: Understanding Seaweed *(Estragon Press) made many people look at that slimy stuff on the beach in a new light. When she tied it together with Irish stout (she uses Black Rock Irish Stout from Dungarvan Brewing), we were sold. When not writing, Sally also leads inspiring kayaking and seaweed foraging trips in West Cork with Atlantic Sea Kayaking. Keep an eye on www.guides.ie – she is also half of the McKennas' Guides team – for more information.*

500g wholewheat flour
3 tablespoons milled dilisk seaweed (you can mill your own in a coffee grinder)
1 teaspoon salt
1 level teaspoon baking soda

500ml stout (or stout and milk mixed)
1 tablespoon barley malt syrup or molasses
5 teaspoons red wine vinegar

Preheat the oven to 200°C. Thoroughly grease a 900g loaf tin.

Mix together the flour, dilisk, salt and baking soda. Make a well in the centre of the flour and add the stout, malt syrup and vinegar. Stir to mix, bringing the mixture together to form a porridge consistency.

Scrape the batter into the loaf tin. It should nearly reach the top. Bake in the oven for 40–45 minutes, or until the tip of a knife inserted into the bread comes out clean. Cool on a wire rack before slicing.

Cheddar, Chive and Red Ale Bread
Makes 1 x 450g loaf

A cheese and beer bread is only as good as the ingredients. This version uses a well-flavoured mature farmhouse Cheddar, like Hegarty's, Coolattin or Mount Callan, along with a red ale from 5 Lamps Brewing, O'Hara's or try Porterhouse. Other variations to play around with are blue cheese, stout (or even a medium-dry cider) and sage; or try goat's cheese, pale ale and thyme.

50g butter, plus extra for greasing
50g strong Cheddar cheese
350g plain flour
1 tablespoon baking powder
1 teaspoon salt
1 teaspoon granulated sugar
handful of finely chopped fresh chives
330ml red ale

Preheat the oven to 190°C (170°C fan). Thoroughly butter and flour the base and sides of a 450g loaf tin.

Melt the butter, grate the cheese and set both aside.

Sift the flour, baking powder and salt into a large bowl. Add the grated cheese, sugar and chives. Mix thoroughly and make a well in the centre. Pour in the ale and stir gently, until just combined.

Scrape into the loaf tin, pour over the melted butter and cook in the oven for 50–60 minutes, until well browned. Slip it out of the tin – if the loaf is ready, the base will sound hollow when you tap it with your knuckles. If not, return it to the oven without the tin for 5 more minutes.

Cool on a wire rack – if you can resist! – before cutting and serving with bowls of chunky lentil soup.

Boozy Bacon Jam

Makes approx. 300g

Ed Hick, a fourth-generation master butcher in Dun Laoghaire, caused quite a buzz when he introduced his bacon jam in 2011 and it soon developed something of a cult following. Food writer Corinna Hardgrave called it Ireland's answer to foie gras and jars of it were snapped up as fast as Ed could make them. Ed's bacon jam has it all: salt (from the bacon), sweetness (onion, maple syrup and sugar), sour (vinegar), bitter (coffee) and umami (slow-cooked meat). Our version, not surprisingly, adds a new twist: Irish craft stout. Ideally you want a stout with a smokier, earthier edge to marry with the smoked bacon as opposed to the more chocolatey stouts. McGrath's Irish Black Stout #4 or Carraig Dubh from Beoir Chorca Dhuibhne would fit the bill.

Try a dollop of bacon jam on eggs, on avocado toast, with roasted or grilled chicken or meaty white fish like cod, haddock or monkfish. It's also a knockout addition to a ploughman's lunch – spread it on oatcakes or Sheridan's brown bread crackers, top with a slice of mature farmhouse Cheddar and be sure to have a craft stout or brown ale to sip alongside.

1 tablespoon sunflower oil
450g smoked rashers, chopped
1 large onion, thickly sliced
3 fat garlic cloves, sliced
300ml stout

75ml balsamic vinegar
100g dark brown sugar
1 tablespoon instant espresso
    powder (optional)

Heat the sunflower oil in a heavy-bottomed pan (one with a lid) over a medium heat. Add in the rashers and raise the heat a little to medium-high. Fry the bacon for 15–20 minutes, until it is completely cooked through and only a little crispy (if it cooks too much, the texture of the final jam will be a little too rough). Resist the urge to stir it around too much and keep a close eye on it for the last 5 minutes of the cooking time, as it can burn easily at the end – you might need to turn the heat down if it is on the verge of being overdone.

Line a plate with kitchen paper and transfer the bacon to the plate with a slotted spoon. Pour off all but 1 tablespoon or so of the bacon fat left behind in the pot (keep the rest in case you need it later on). Reduce the heat to low and add in the sliced onions. Give them a stir so that they are all coated with the fat, adding in a little more if the pot looks too dry. Cover with a lid and gently sauté for about 10 minutes, stirring now and then to check on them, until they have softened but not browned. Add in the garlic and cook, uncovered, for 1–2 minutes more, just until the garlic is fragrant and has lost its raw edge.

Add in a splash of the stout to deglaze the pot, making sure to scrape up any browned bits that have stuck to the bottom. Add the drained bacon back to the pot along with the rest of the stout, the balsamic vinegar, brown sugar and espresso powder (if using), stirring to melt the sugar. Bring to the boil, but don't lean too close over the pot unless you want to get a sinus-clearing blast of vinegar fumes. Reduce the heat to low and let it simmer gently, uncovered, for about 1 hour, until the liquid has reduced to a thick, syrupy glaze. Take it off the heat before the liquid reduces too much, though, since it will continue to thicken a little as it cools.

Transfer to a clean jam jar or airtight container and store in the fridge. It will probably keep for a week or two, but we can't say for sure because it is always long gone before then.

Hooker and Highbank Mustard
Makes 4 x 200ml jars

New Zealander Jess Murphy brings a fresh eye to Irish ingredients at her Kai Café and Restaurant in Galway. The chef/proprietor engages with and showcases the best of local produce, taking no shortcuts and displaying plenty of Kiwi flair on the menu. When we spotted this mustard recipe in The Irish Times, *using products from no fewer than three small producers, it went straight on our must-make list. Jess uses Galway Hooker, but any craft pale ale would work. It is also well worth trying with red ale or even a stout. If your mustard seeds are proving difficult to blend (older seeds can be slow to soften), let them soak for longer. Ours took two days and a hand-held blender to turn them into a paste.*

350g golden mustard seeds
500ml Galway Hooker pale ale
350ml cider vinegar
6 tablespoons Highbank Orchard Syrup
1 teaspoon Achill Island sea salt
1 teaspoon ground mace or nutmeg
pinch of chilli flakes

Mix the mustard seeds and ale together in a bowl, cover and soak overnight.

The next day, sterilise your jars. If you have a dishwasher, you can simply run everything through a hot cycle. Otherwise, wash everything in hot, soapy water, rinse well, then place the jars and lids on a baking tray in an oven heated to 140°C to dry them.

Stir the remaining ingredients into the mustard seeds. Blend in small batches in a food processor until nearly smooth. Spoon into the sterilised jars to within a few millimetres of the rim and tap gently to remove air bubbles. Seal immediately. Leave for at least 3 weeks or up to a month to mature. Store in a cool, dry place.

N17 Spent Grain Granola Bars
Makes 12–16 bars

When grain is mashed in the beer-making process, the brewers are only interested in the water it was steeped in – the wort. The grains have given up most of their sugars to the beer in this process, so spent grains often get used as compost, animal feed or even as a medium for growing mushrooms.

But you can also use spent grain in a variety of ways in your kitchen. It can be incorporated into bread and baking, added to home-made pasta or tortillas, dried and whizzed to a flour, used to bulk up veggie burgers, included in energy bars or even used in home-made dog treats. Home brewers have a variety of creative ways of coping with this by-product, showing that a brewer's trash can be a home cook's treasure.

Sarah Roarty from the N17 Brewery sees beer as the pinnacle of a cascading range of products, and strives to get as much value as possible from every part of the brewing process in order to 'squeeze every last drop out'. She makes granola bars from her spent grains – the batch she brought along to the 2014 Alltech International Craft Brews and Food Fair disappeared in record time, along with her medal-winning oatmeal stout. Should you be doing some home brewing or know a friendly brewer, here is her recipe. You will see that Sarah uses cups instead of weighing the ingredients – you can use whatever teacup or mug you have at home.

2 cups spent grain
1 cup rolled porridge oats
½ cup flaked almonds
½ cup desiccated coconut
2 cups honey
¼ cup light brown sugar
3 tablespoons butter

decent pinch of salt
½ cup dried fruits of your choice
   (apricots, cranberries, dates)
½ cup nuts of your choice,
   roughly chopped (almonds,
   pecans, walnuts)

Preheat the oven to 80°C. Spread the spent grain out on a baking tray and dry in the oven for 2 hours, stirring occasionally.

In the meantime, grease a 30cm x 20cm baking tray, line it with parchment paper and leave it aside, ready for the granola bar mixture.

When the spent grains have finished drying out, increase the oven temperature to 180°C. On a separate baking sheet (not the greased and lined one), mix together the porridge oats, flaked almonds and coconut and bake for 10–12 minutes, until lightly browned and toasted.

Combine the honey, brown sugar, butter and salt in a large pan and bring to the boil over a medium heat for 1 minute, stirring all the time. Remove from the heat, then stir in the spent grain and toasted oat, almond and coconut mixture. Add the dried fruit and nuts and stir well.

Wet your fingers or use the back of a large serving spoon and press the mixture firmly and evenly into the prepared baking tray. Bake for 20 minutes, until set. Cool for 1–2 hours before cutting into squares – but don't leave it for too long before you cut them unless you have an angle grinder handy! Enjoy with a glass of your favourite brew.

Baked Irish Brie with
Red Ale Caramel and Pecans
Serves 4

This is a simple – if rich! – starter for four. Caroline also likes it as an after-the-kids-go-to-bed feast for two in front of a roaring fire. Try making it with McGrath's Irish Red Ale #1, Porterhouse Red or Clotworthy Dobbin from the Whitewater Brewery.

1 small wheel of Cooleeney Brie
   (approx. 200g)
75g dark brown sugar

3 tablespoons red ale
50g pecans, toasted
freshly ground black pepper

Preheat the oven to 200°C (180°C fan).

Put the Brie in an ovenproof dish and cut a cross into the top of the rind. Put it into the oven and bake for 15–20 minutes, until the cheese is soft and runny in the middle. Remove from the oven.

Meanwhile, put the brown sugar and ale into a heavy-based saucepan and melt the sugar over a medium heat. Simmer for 4–5 minutes, until syrupy. Add the pecans and stir well. Add plenty of coarsely ground black pepper and remove from the heat.

Pull the cut rind back from the top of the warm cheese, pour the caramel sauce and pecans over and dive in! Serve warm with crusty bread or cheese crackers, thin slices of pear or apple – and teaspoons.

Double Chocolate Porter Brownies
Makes 30 brownies

This is becoming the brownie that has launched a thousand demos. Caroline developed it for a cookery demonstration in the RDS when Eight Degrees Brewing brought out their first batch of Knockmealdown Porter. Since then it has become one of her favourite go-to baking-with-beer recipes, whether brought along to Foodcamp tastings in Kilkenny, served at the end of beer and food pairing events or almost creating a stampede when served at the Electric Picnic's Theatre of Food.

A dark, full-bodied porter or stout provides a good balance to the chocolate in these brownies. Caroline uses Knockmealdown Porter from Eight Degrees Brewing, but Dungarvan Black Rock Irish Stout, Porterhouse Plain or O'Hara's Irish Stout are all well worth trying. You only need 250ml, so there will be a little left over to accompany the baked brownies – if you don't drink it while doing the washing up!

100g plain flour
50g cocoa
½ teaspoon baking powder
¼ teaspoon salt
175g butter

150g dark chocolate (50–60% cocoa solids)
200g caster sugar
2 eggs
250ml porter or stout
½ teaspoon vanilla extract

Preheat the oven to 180°C (fan 160°C). Line a rectangular 25cm x 30cm Swiss roll tin with greaseproof paper.

Sift the flour, cocoa, baking powder and salt together and set aside.

Gently melt the butter and chocolate together in a large, heavy-based saucepan over a low heat. Take it off the heat and add the sugar, whisking until smooth. Allow to cool slightly, then whisk in the eggs, porter, vanilla and finally the sifted dry ingredients until just blended.

Pour into the prepared tin – this is a very runny mixture – and bake in the oven for 18–20 minutes, until set and a skewer inserted into the middle comes out clean. Because of the amount of liquid used, you don't need to underbake these brownies.

Cool in the tin, then cut into 30 pieces and store – if you have any left – in an airtight container. These get more moist the longer you keep them, but they never hang around for too long.

White Chocolate, Raspberry and Pale Ale Blondies
Makes 25 blondies

While a lot of Caroline's baking is done with porter and dark chocolate, sometimes there is a treat to be made and nothing to be found in the kitchen but Howling Gale pale ale, white chocolate and, serendipitously, a punnet of raspberries. Try these with Galway Bay Brewery's Bay Ale or Deception Golden Ale from Trouble Brewing.

125g white chocolate
150g plain flour
1½ teaspoons baking powder
½ teaspoon salt
175g caster sugar
125g butter, at room temperature
2 eggs
60ml natural yoghurt
60ml pale ale
175g raspberries

For the white chocolate glaze:
75g white chocolate, roughly
    chopped
50ml cream
1 tablespoon pale ale
pinch of salt

Preheat the oven to 180°C (fan 160°C). Line a 23cm square cake tin with greaseproof paper.

Put the chocolate in a heatproof bowl set over a pot of simmering water (a bain-marie), making sure the chocolate never comes into direct contact with the water. Melt the chocolate and leave to cool. Sift the flour, baking powder and salt together in a medium bowl.

Using an electric mixer, beat the sugar and butter together until pale and fluffy. Beat in the eggs, one at a time, along with 1 tablespoon of flour if the mixture looks like it is curdling. Mix in the yoghurt, then the dry ingredients, the ale and the melted chocolate. Finally, gently fold in the raspberries.

Scrape into the prepared tin and bake for 40–45 minutes, until firm, golden brown and a cake tester comes out clean. Allow to cool on a wire rack.

To make the glaze, place the chopped chocolate in a small bowl. Bring the cream and ale just to the boil, then pour it over the chopped chocolate and stir until melted and smooth. Add the salt and cool for about 1 hour in the fridge, until thickened, before drizzling generously over the cold cake. Allow the glaze to set before slicing into 25 pieces.

Chocolate Porter Cake
Serves 8–10

This recipe started out as a chocolate cola celebration cake from Nessa Robins's beautiful debut cookbook, Apron Strings. *But leave it to a brewer's other half to swap out the cola for the porter that is always on hand, which is exactly what Caroline did. Two to try are Trouble Brewing's Dark Arts Porter or Galway Bay Brewery's Buried at Sea Chocolate Milk Stout. If you want to try the original version, just use cola in place of the porter. You could also crown this with a chocolate porter ganache: finely chop 150g of dark chocolate and put it in a small heatproof bowl. Bring 150ml of cream and 2 tablespoons of porter to the boil, then pour it over the chocolate and stir until melted and smooth. Allow to cool before spreading thickly over the top of the cake.*

Preheat the oven to 200°C (fan 180°C). Prepare a 26cm cake tin by lightly greasing the sides and placing a disk of parchment on the base.

250g chocolate (at least 50% cocoa solids)
150g butter
150ml porter or stout

6 eggs
175g caster sugar
cream or ice cream, to serve

Place the chocolate, butter and porter into a medium-sized saucepan over a low heat. Stir continuously until the butter and chocolate have melted and the mixture is smooth and silky. Remove from the heat.

Using an electric mixer and a large bowl, whisk the eggs and sugar together for 5–7 minutes, until it is light and foamy. Slowly pour in the chocolate mixture and gently fold through. Pour into the prepared tin. Bake in the preheated oven for 30–40 minutes. The outside will be crisp with some moistness in the centre.

Remove the cake from the oven and leave to cool completely in its tin on a wire rack. Once cold, remove the cake from the tin and place onto a serving plate. Don't worry if the cake collapses in the centre or cracks a little – simply cover it up with some chocolate porter ganache (see note above). Serve with a dollop of cream or ice cream.

Pale Ale Cookies (*Hojarascas*)
Makes 20 cookies

Julia Child famously said, 'If you're afraid of butter, use cream.' These days, she might say you should use lard – it's the new white gold after decades of being off limits. Expat Lily Ramirez-Foran says that Mexicans have been using lard for cooking and baking for centuries. The best-quality pork lard will give you amazing pastry, and in this case it gives the cookies a beautiful texture and enhances the flavour of the beer. If you are still nervous about using it or if you can't get it, you can substitute it with the same amount of butter. The flavour and texture will be different, but it will still be a tasty treat nonetheless. And if you are wondering what the pale ale adds to these cookies, it imparts a biscuity flavour and acts as the raising agent too. Galway Hooker would work well, as would a toasty, bready pilsner such as Eight Degrees Barefoot Bohemian.

If you want to get your hands on some lard, Ed Hick sells it at the Killruddery House and Temple Bar farmers' markets (though you might tweet him first @edhick to make sure he will have it before you go), or you can contact Margaret O'Farrell at Oldfarm (www.oldfarm.ie) and order a jar or two of lard made from her own free-range pigs. If you are looking for authentic Mexican ingredients, be sure to check out Lily's shop, Picado Mexican, or her blog, A Mexican Cook (www.amexicancook.ie), for even more recipes. Her cochinita pibil, salsas and margaritas are legendary.

For the cookies:
250g cream flour
100g pork lard or chilled butter, diced
30g caster sugar
25g Cookeen (vegetable fat), chilled and diced
25g pecans, finely chopped
1/8 teaspoon salt
150ml pale ale

For the sugary coating:
40g caster sugar
2 teaspoons ground cinnamon

Preheat the oven to 180°C and get 2 baking trays ready. There is no need to grease them; the fat in these cookies means they won't stick.

Prepare the sugary coating by mixing the caster sugar and cinnamon in a shallow bowl. Set aside to use later.

Put the flour, lard, sugar, Cookeen, chopped pecans and salt in a large bowl and mix the ingredients with your hands, rubbing in the fats with your fingertips. Pour the beer over the dry ingredients and mix it all up with your hands to form a dough, taking care not to overwork the dough or the cookies will be tough. A light touch is the key here. The dough should be soft, smooth and damp, but not sticky. If the dough isn't coming together (it can happen if the weather is cold or damp – which means it can often happen in Ireland), add a tiny bit more beer. Bear in mind that the heat of your hands will soften the fats, making the dough more pliable and easier to work. Knead it just enough to bring it all together into a smooth ball, exactly like you would if you were making scones.

Transfer the dough to a lightly floured surface and roll into a circle about 5mm thick (flour the rolling pin to keep the dough from sticking to it). Using your favourite cookie cutter or a scone cutter (a round 5cm one works well), stamp out the cookies from the dough and lay them on the baking tray.

Bake in the preheated oven for 18–20 minutes. The cookies must be golden brown on the bottom, but they don't need to be fully brown on the top. As soon as the cookies are out of the oven, dip them in the sugar coating you prepared earlier, making sure every cookie is well covered. Cool on a wire rack.

These cookies keep well in an airtight container for up to 5 days. They are light, crumbly and very tasty – perfect with a cold glass of milk or a nice cup of tea.

Stout Marshmallows

Makes 40–50 large marshmallows

Cloud Confectionary's Sarah Galvin makes the freshest, most imaginative marshmallows you will ever taste. Close your eyes and think of biting into a light, sweet cloud of marshmallow flavoured with raspberry ripple, minty mojito or salted caramel shortbread. Sarah also uses beer to make properly grown-up marshmallows that are too good to share with the kids. Try them dipped into a chocolate ganache: heat 50ml of cream and pour it over 50g of finely chopped dark chocolate. Stir. Dip marshmallows. Eat. Repeat. The beer flavour is quite prominent in these marshmallows, so something that has chocolate notes, like Galway Bay Brewery's Buried at Sea Milk Chocolate Stout or Trouble Brewing's Dark Arts Porter, would work well. Sarah has also made a version with Dungarvan Brewing's seasonal Coffee and Oatmeal Stout. You can find Cloud Confectionary on Twitter at @CloudMallows.

vegetable oil, for greasing
4 tablespoons icing sugar
4 tablespoons cornflour
300ml stout

25g powdered gelatine
440g caster sugar
160g golden syrup

Lightly oil a 23cm square baking tin. Mix together the icing sugar and cornflour and dust the tin with about a tablespoon of this mixture.

Pour 100ml of the stout into the bowl of a stand mixer fitted with the whisk attachment and sprinkle over the powdered gelatine. Give it a stir and leave to bloom.

Meanwhile, pour the remaining 200ml of beer into a heavy-based pan and stir in the sugar and golden syrup. Using a candy thermometer, gently heat to the firm ball stage (120°C). This won't take long – just long enough for the sugar to melt and turn syrupy – so don't wander off. If it gets too hot, take the pan off the heat and let it cool down until it is the right temperature.

Turn on the mixer to low. Being very careful – hot sugar can badly burn you – slowly pour this mixture into the gelatine bloom. Once it has thickened a little, gradually increase the speed to high and whisk for 8– 10 minutes, until the mixture has trebled in volume and become a bit like a meringue, has turned a light latte colour and holds its shape slightly as it falls off the whisk.

Pour into the prepared tin and leave to set, uncovered, at room temperature for a few hours. Sift a little more of the icing sugar and cornflour mixture over the top, then prise the slab of marshmallow out of the tin and cut into 3cm squares with a sharp knife. Sift a little more of the icing sugar and cornflour mixture over the freshly cut sides.

The marshmallows can be stored in an airtight container, but they are best enjoyed when very fresh. Their texture starts to change as the days go by, but keeping them in the fridge helps to maintain the texture for longer.

Cider Sorbet

Proving that there is a place for top-quality craft beer and cider even at a Michelin-starred table, this cider sorbet was created for the Irish Food Writers' Guild Food Awards 2014 by chefs Derry Clarke and Michael Hunter of l'Ecrivain Restaurant in Dublin. It was developed to showcase Stonewell Cider, which won the Guild's first ever drink award, by contrasting the cider's tangy flavours with a sweet and salty mousse and a salted caramel in a contemporary Irish dessert. If you would like to see the recipe for the entire trio, it's on the Irish Food Writers' Guild website (www.irishfoodwritersguild.ie).

The original recipe calls for the sorbet to be made in an ice cream maker, but don't despair if you don't have one. Once the mixture is fully frozen, whizz it in a food processor, then put it back in the freezer in an airtight container. It won't be as smooth as a sorbet made in a machine, but it will do the trick. Or you could even make it as a granita: pour the mixture into a shallow tray and place it in the freezer. Every half hour or so, stir it with a fork. Continue until it is frozen solid and rough crystals have formed. Use whatever style of cider you like best (dry, medium or sweet) for this recipe.

250g caster sugar
125ml water
1 teaspoon glucose syrup
150g pressed apple juice (the
    apple juice needs to be
    weighed)

500ml Irish craft cider
juice of 1 lemon

Bring the sugar, water and glucose syrup to the boil, then turn down the heat and simmer for 3 minutes. Remove from the heat and add the remaining ingredients. Leave to cool, then churn in an ice cream maker according to the manufacturer's instructions.

Irish Red Ale and Elderflower Ice Pops
Makes 4 x 50ml ice pops

You don't really need a recipe for this one, just some good-quality beer and elderflower cordial. Depending on the strength of the cordial used, you might need a little more than the amount mentioned in the recipe. Just make sure that the mixture tastes good and strong before you freeze it, as freezing dulls some of the flavour. Not the alcohol, though – these ice pops are strictly for grown-ups!

180ml red ale
25–30ml elderflower cordial, or to taste

Measure beer. Pour in cordial. Mix well. Taste. Consider. Realise that it needs another tasting. Fill ice pop moulds with what's left. Leaving room for expansion, freeze overnight. Finish the rest of the beer while you are waiting. Carefully remove from the moulds and enjoy in the sun.

Part four

LAST CALL

CHAPTER 9

RESOURCES AND EVENTS

RESOURCES

Beer Academy

www.beeracademy.co.uk

Based in London but offering occasional courses in Dublin too, the Beer Academy is an operating arm of the Institute of Brewing and Distilling and aims to help people to understand, appreciate and enjoy beer sensibly. They run courses on how to judge beer and become a beer sommelier, and they teach beer and food matching too.

Beer Judge Certification Program

www.bjcp.org

Founded in 1985, the BJCP works to promote beer literacy and the appreciation of real beer and to recognise beer tasting and evaluation skills. They certify and rank beer judges through an examination and monitoring process, which is now available in Ireland (and elsewhere throughout Europe). Their website is also an excellent resource if you want to familiarise yourself with the characteristics of a variety of beer and cider styles.

Beoir

www.beoir.org

Established in 2010, Beoir (*beoir* is the Gaelic word for beer) is an independent group of beer-loving consumers who aim to support and raise awareness of Ireland's independent microbreweries and cider-makers. Beoir also promotes and encourages amateur craft brewing by sharing information. Membership is open to all adults worldwide and costs €10 per annum. They maintain a comprehensive directory on their website of all the independent Irish microbreweries and cider-makers as well as a list of all the pubs and bars, off-licenses, brewpubs and restaurants that stock craft beer and cider, which is updated regularly. Beoir has also produced the BeoirFinder app, which is basically their directory, but in an easy-to-use app format. The website also features articles, reviews, home brewing tips and info, a calendar of festivals and events, a chat room and other helpful links.

Brewery Hops of Ireland

www.breweryhopsofireland.com

Offering a one-, three- or five-day tour of Irish microbreweries, this is the perfect holiday for beer lovers. The tour starts and finishes in Dublin but focuses on the south-west of the country, where you'll visit microbreweries and the Kilbeggan distillery, meet the brewers and sample their ales, lagers and stouts, visit a few heritage sites and spend your evenings experiencing the music and atmosphere of Irish pubs serving good food – and have great *craic* while doing so.

CAMRA Northern Ireland

www.camrani.org.uk

With over 300 members, CAMRA has been active in Northern Ireland since 1981 and leads the campaign for real ale there through monthly meetings and social and campaigning events throughout the year. They are the volunteer organisers of the annual Belfast Beer and Cider Festival (see page 203) and produce *The Ulster Ale* branch magazine, available in pubs throughout the province or to download via their website. They also maintain a list of craft breweries, real ale pubs and real ale stockists on their website. Membership is open to those living in Northern Ireland who love real ale and real cider.

Cider Ireland

www.ciderireland.com

Cider Ireland is a group of like-minded craft cider producers from the island of Ireland who want to ensure the quality and integrity of the Irish craft cider industry as it moves forward. Their website includes a directory of members of artisan cider-makers and apple-growers who adhere to a set of criteria and is a hub for info on upcoming tastings and events as well as recent press reviews. Members are also allowed to use the Cider Ireland quality mark on their produce.

Craft Beer Ireland
www.craftbeer.ie

Maintained by this book's authors, Caroline Hennessy and Kristin Jensen, Craft Beer Ireland aims to be the go-to source of information about all things related to Irish craft beer and cider. Follow them on Facebook and Twitter (@CraftBeer_ie) to keep up to date with all the latest brew news.

DrinkAware.ie
www.drinkaware.ie

Launched in 2006, the overall aim of the drinkaware.ie initiative is to promote the responsible use of alcohol. The website is full of tips, facts, downloadable publications, competitions and a standard drinks calculator.

Dublin Ladies Craft Beer Society

The mission of the Dublin Ladies Craft Beer Society is to foster the love of all things craft beer. Whether you are an experienced beer aficionado or a novice pint drinker, there is an event for everyone. Members go to beer tastings, beer festivals, brewery tours and beer dinners. The society also hosts educational events about home brewing and beer styles to assist and promote women who want to further their knowledge of the topic. They endeavour to show new women drinkers that beer is not a one-flavour-note catch-all and to create an environment where experienced craft beer lovers can meet and swap notes with other like-minded women.

Independent Craft Brewers of Ireland
www.icbi.ie

The ICBI is a voluntary association, chaired by Seamus O'Hara of Carlow Brewing with secretary Cuilán Loughnane, which was set up in 2013 to foster the spirit of co-operation within the sector. Independently owned microbreweries in Ireland that produce less than 20,000hl per annum (as set out by the Revenue Commissioners) are eligible to join. The ICBI is working on a mark of origin for Irish craft beer so that consumers can be assured that their beer is brewed here in Ireland.

Institute of Brewing and Distilling

www.ibd.org.uk

Based in the UK, the IBD offers a Diploma in Brewing, which is a necessary prerequisite for taking their Master Brewer Exam and carries NFQ Level 6 accreditation in Ireland. Organised into three modules (Materials and Wort; Yeast and Beer; Packaging and Process Technology), the diploma is run as a combination of online distance learning and in-person tutorials and revision, which are held at locations in Ireland as well as the UK. The brewing courses in Ireland are being organised by Skillnet using an IBD accredited trainer, Tim O'Rourke. Check www.taste4success.ie for more information.

Irish Seed Savers Association

www.irishseedsavers.ie

Founded in 1991, the ISSA does invaluable work to preserve Ireland's food heritage and biodiversity. They cultivate around 600 heirloom vegetable varieties, almost 50 heirloom grain varieties, 140 native apple varieties and an heirloom potato collection. If you are interested in growing a heritage apple variety (perhaps with an eye to making your own cider), you need look no further than the ISSA catalogue.

National Homebrew Club Ireland

www.nationalhomebrewclub.com

Founded in 2011, the National Homebrew Club is run by home brewers for home brewers, and acts as an umbrella organisation for regional home brewing groups. Some of their objectives are to organise brewing demos and other activities, to offer discounted pricing on home brewing materials via group buys and to provide a pooled wiki of brewing knowledge specific to Ireland. They also organise the National Brewing Championships, Ireland's biggest home brewing competition, and run a beer judge certification programme.

Online Retailers

Despite the growing popularity of craft beer and cider, it can be hard to find it outside of the main cities and large towns. Luckily, there are several online retailers (and all independent, family-run businesses at that) who will deliver nationwide for a small charge – a great way to stock up.

- **Bradley's:** Check out the huge range available at Cork's specialist off-licence and food store, established in 1850 and now in its fourth generation as a family business. They currently stock around 500 beers and the selection continues to grow. www.bradleysofflicence.ie
- **Drinkstore:** This family-run independent off-licence offers Irish and world craft beers as well as cider, perry, wines, liqueurs, spirits and more. www.drinkstore.ie
- **Martins Off-Licence:** Offers a large selection of Irish and international beers as well as wine, spirits and hampers. Their website includes food and wine matching tips. www.martinsofflicence.ie
- **McHugh's Off-Licence:** Winner of the National Beer Specialist Award eleven times since 2000, the online beer selection is searchable by style or country. Wines, spirits and gifts are also available. www.mchughs.ie
- **The Beer Box:** Operated by Deveney's of Dundrum (organisers of the Secret Beer Garden Festival; see page 207), this unique site offers a selection of hampers made up of beers, snacks and glassware. www.beerbox.ie
- **The Beer Club:** Stocking over 400 craft beers from Ireland and around the world, the Beer Club specialises in craft beer hampers and membership plans. They also offer home brewing classes and supplies and run off-site beer tastings. www.thebeerclub.ie

If you're looking for thoughtful, articulate writing on beer in Ireland, you'll find it in the blogosphere. These people are beer lovers, some are home brewers, several are involved in Beoir and if you want an honest review of a new beer, this is where you'll find it. Five to bookmark: Beers I've Known, The Beer Nut, The Drunken Destrier, The Irish Beer Snob, The Tale of the Ale.

Also check out Doerthe Woltermann's capital-orientated beer blog on Lovin' Dublin and the unmissable 11pm Somewhere podcasts for entertainingly opinionated musings on Irish craft beer.

> *'Whoever drinks beer, he is quick to sleep; whoever sleeps long, does not sin; whoever does not sin, enters Heaven! Thus, let us drink beer!'*
> *– Martin Luther*

FESTIVALS AND EVENTS

With the ever-increasing popularity of craft beer and cider, new beer festivals are being organised all the time and many food festivals or community festivals now include a craft beer and cider element. The following are the most established annual festivals, but be sure to log on to the Craft Beer Ireland website (www.craftbeer.ie) for the most up-to-date listing of festivals and events.

A festival year

February: Alltech International Craft Brews and Food Fair, Franciscan Well Winter Ales and Cask Ales Festival

March: Irish Craft Beer and Food Market

April: Franciscan Well Easterfest (a movable feast, depending on Easter!)

May: Secret Beer Garden Festival

June: Bloom – The Bloom Inn

July: Great Northern Irish Beer and Cider Festival

August: Annascaul Beerfest, Dirty Duck Ale Festival, Hilden Beer and Music Festival, Irish Craft Beer Festival – Doolin

September: Irish Craft Beer and Cider Festival, Slow Food Apple and Craft Cider Festival

November: Belfast Beer and Cider Festival

Alltech International Craft Brews and Food Fair

Where: Dublin | **When:** February/March
www.alltechbrewsandfood.com

Alltech arrived on the Irish craft beer scene with a bang. They have plans to open a craft brewing academy by the end of 2014 and to launch a new distillery in an old church on James's Street in Dublin. Meanwhile, their annual fair showcases some of the best craft beer from Ireland and abroad, as well as Irish artisan food producers. Live music, demos and talks feature too, aimed at both casual beer fans and industry pros.

Annascaul Beerfest

Where: Annascaul, Co. Kerry | **When:** August bank holiday weekend
annascaulbeerfest.wordpress.com

This is a beer festival with a difference, as proceeds go to charity. Organised by the people and publicans of the village of Annascaul in West Kerry, the festival is held over the August bank holiday weekend and features music and other events, such as beer and food pairings, BBQs or a road race.

Belfast Beer and Cider Festival

Where: Ulster Hall, Belfast | **When:** November
www.belfastbeerfestival.co.uk

Organised by a team of volunteers from CAMRA Northern Ireland (see page 198), this festival, launched in 1999, features over 100 real ales, ciders and perries. They also offer tutored tasting sessions in small groups, but book early – those tend to sell out.

Bloom – The Bloom Inn

Where: Phoenix Park, Dublin | **When:** June bank holiday weekend
www.bloominthepark.com

Bloom is a hugely successful gardening and food festival held in Dublin's Phoenix Park every June bank holiday, drawing over 100,000 visitors in recent years. The Bloom Inn is a popular part of the Food Village, offering craft beers and spirits. You can meet the brewers and sample their beers, which are available to enjoy on site or to take home with you – why not try matching them with the artisan foods from the festival?

Dirty Duck Ale Festival

Where: The Dirty Duck Alehouse, Holywood, Co. Down
When: UK August bank holiday weekend
www.thedirtyduckalehouse.co.uk

Mark McCrory was the first person to import cask ale into Northern Ireland, and his gastropub, the Dirty Duck Ale House in Holywood, outside Belfast, has ten or eleven different casks on the go every week. For their annual festival, though, they bring in thirty-five to forty different cask ales. Well worth going out of your way for if you love cask ale.

Franciscan Well Easterfest

Where: Franciscan Well Brewery, Cork City | **When:** Easter weekend
www.franciscanwellbrewery.com

One of the longest-running beer festivals, this is a highlight of the beer festival year. You can sample up to thirty Irish craft ales, lagers, stouts and wheat beers as well as cask ales in a heated outdoor area, with seriously good pizza on site from Pompeii Pizza's wood-fired oven.

Franciscan Well Winter Ales and Cask Ales Festival

Where: Franciscan Well Brewery, Cork City | **When:** February
www.franciscanwellbrewery.com

One of the first events of the year, this wintertime festival celebrates cask ales and seasonal winter beers from Ireland's microbreweries.

Great Northern Irish Beer and Cider Festival

Where: The John Hewitt, Belfast | **When:** July
www.thejohnhewitt.com

This festival, held in the award-winning John Hewitt pub in Belfast, is unique in that it focuses solely on craft beers and ciders produced in Northern Ireland. The pub is also renowned for its live music, which is a feature of the festival too.

Hilden Beer and Music Festival

Where: Hilden Brewery, Lisburn, Co. Antrim
When: UK August bank holiday weekend
www.taproomhilden.com

Beer festivals are becoming increasingly popular, but Hilden Brewery was a pioneer when they established this long-running festival in 1984. Held in the Georgian stable courtyard of the Hilden Brewery, this is an event for craft beer aficionados as well as music-lovers, featuring over thirty-five craft beers and ciders from the UK and Ireland and more than twenty music acts over the UK's August bank holiday weekend. The Tap Room Restaurant fires up the BBQ to offer burgers, hot dogs and steak sandwiches made with local produce too. Families are welcome on the Sunday of the festival, with attractions such as face painting, magicians, balloon artists and a bouncy castle in addition to the food, music and, of course, beer.

Irish Craft Beer and Cider Festival

Where: RDS, Dublin | **When:** September
www.irishcraftbeerfestival.com

A celebration of Irish craft brewing, cider-making, whiskey, live music and artisan Irish food, this is the star of the beer festival year. Approximately forty brewers and 100 different beers and ciders are featured, some of which are only available as one-offs at the festival. Several masterclasses and interactive sessions are organised too. An app is available to help you navigate your way through the festival, including a listing of the brewers and beers, complete with tasting notes (search for 'Irish Craft Beer and Cider Festival' in the app store, as it is updated every year). If you want to see the biggest and best range of what Irish craft beer and cider has to offer, this is the place – not to be missed!

Irish Craft Beer and Food Market

Where: IFSC, Dublin | **When:** March
www.irishfest.ie

Organised by the same people who run the Irish Craft Beer and Cider Festival in September, the Village forms part of the wider St Patrick's Festival celebrations. Irish beer and cider as well as artisan food and live music are all on offer at the IFSC in Dublin.

Irish Craft Beer Festival – Doolin

Where: Doolin, Co. Clare | **When:** August
www.irishcraftbeerfestival.com

The sister festival of the main Irish Craft Beer and Cider Festival in the RDS in Dublin, this is a small-scale event in the grounds of Hotel Doolin, which has even launched their very own Dooliner Beer (brewed by C&C), which is popular with both tourists and locals. In addition to the craft beer, artisan and local food and live music, other events might include beer and cheese tastings or a farmers' market.

Secret Beer Garden Festival

Where: Dundrum Town Centre, Dundrum, Dublin | **When:** May
www.beerfestival.ie

Organised by retailer Deveney's of Dundrum, this festival is all about variety, with hundreds of beers from around the world. Beer is served in small 150ml portions so that you can taste a wide range of beers and styles from many different countries, including Irish beers.

Slow Food Apple and Craft Cider Festival

Where: Location changes | **When:** September
www.slowfoodireland.com

Billing itself as a celebration of apples and all things made from apples, this festival is a wonderful chance to sample Irish and international craft ciders. You can expect food, music, family activities, competitions, guided tours, workshops and demos, such as apple-pressing and cider-making.

---

scoop
n. (colloq.), pint. 'We had a few scoops and went home.'
– A Dictionary of Hiberno-English, *edited by Terence Patrick Dolan*
(2013)

How to Make the Most of a Beer Festival

Beer festivals are about meeting brewers and sampling new beers and flavours, not getting hammered. If you want to make the most of your time at a festival there are a few things you should do, but the most important thing is just to pace yourself. As ever, always drink responsibly and have a designated driver or other safe way to get home.

1. Eat. It is just common sense that you shouldn't rock up to a beer festival with an empty stomach. Most festivals have some kind of food offering – and increasingly these days, it is top-rate artisan or local food at that – but it is still a good idea to have some food before you go or to have some snacks (or something more substantial if you need it) while you are there.

2. Drink water. Try to alternate your alcoholic drinks with some water. Aim for one water for every two or three beers to keep hydrated and to break down the alcohol in your system.

3. Take your time. Take your time to really savour and appreciate the beers (see Chapter 3 for tips on how to taste beers). There is no rush – you have probably paid for a ticket and are at the festival to try lots of new beers, so you will likely be there for a good few hours anyway. Relax and enjoy the music or other events that might be happening. And who says you have to finish every drink? If you are there to make notes or try lots of new beers, then you only need a couple of sips. Finally, bear in mind that the Department of Health and Children recommends that no more than five standard drinks should be had on any one occasion, and that your body gets rid of roughly one standard drink per hour.

4. Plan ahead. Check the festival website to see if they have a list of the brewers and/or beers that will be available. If they do, then you can decide ahead of time which brewers you most want to talk to or which beers you want to try, especially if there will be one-off specials just for that particular festival that you don't want to miss. The Irish Craft Beer and Cider Festival produces a handy app, including tasting notes for each beer, with space for your own notes too, which could be used for other festivals. Keep in mind that brewers can sell out, so you might want to go towards the start of the festival rather than on the last day.

5. Bring cash. As with almost any festival or farmers' market, bring plenty of cash, especially since some of the smaller festivals might not have an ATM nearby.

---

1 standard drink =

- A glass of stout/lager/cider (284ml)
- A small glass of wine (100ml)
- A pub measure of spirits (35.5ml)

Your body gets rid of roughly one standard drink per hour. Time is the only cure.

The Department of Health and Children advises that up to eleven standard drinks a week for women and up to seventeen standard drinks a week for men is considered low risk. It is important that they are spread out over the week and not saved for one session or big night out, and that no more than five standard drinks are consumed in one sitting.

Source: www.drinkaware.ie

GLOSSARY

ABV: Alcohol by volume, a standard measurement used worldwide of how much alcohol is in a drink. ABV is the number of millilitres of pure ethanol in 100ml of solution at 20°C. It is given as a percentage (the percentage of the drink that is pure alcohol). In craft brewing, higher ABV beers tend to be from the brewers using a lot more malted barley, which in turn can lead to slightly sweeter and more full-bodied beers than beers with a low ABV.

adjunct: According to the Institute of Brewing and Distilling in London, an adjunct is 'any carbohydrate source other than malt that contributes fermentable sugars to the wort (usually less expensive than barley malt)'. See also page 10.

aftertaste: Also known as finish, this is the taste that lingers in your mouth after you eat or drink something. See also page 53.

astringent: One of the possible components of the mouthfeel of a beer, astringency is a sharp, bitter, mouth-puckering taste that can also dry out your palate. See also *mouthfeel*.

barley: A cereal grain that is the main ingredient in beer, the others being hops, yeast and water. See also pages 7–10.

barrel-aged: Ageing beer in wooden wine or spirit barrels is a hot trend in craft beer. Barrel ageing develops complex, multi-layered flavours as the beer rubs shoulders with the wood, adopting the flavours of the wine or spirit that was in the barrel before it.

body: Body is one aspect of the mouthfeel of a beer, and refers to its weight or fullness (how heavy or light it feels in your mouth). Beer can be light bodied (like a lager), medium bodied (such as an IPA) or full bodied (like a doppelbock). Sweeter beers are more full bodied than light-bodied beers because they have more residual sugars. See also *mouthfeel*.

bottle-conditioned: Bottle-conditioned beer undergoes an additional fermentation and conditioning in the bottle, resulting in a naturally carbonated beer. Bottle-conditioned beers are usually labelled as such, but you will be able to tell at a glance if you see a thin layer of sediment in the bottom of the bottle. See also *real ale*.

bottom-fermenting: Strains of yeast that work best at cooler temperatures (7°C to 15°C) and work at the bottom of the fermenter. The beer needs to be finished by storing it at a low temperature, producing a clean, crisp beer (such as lager).

brew kettle: The container that wort is boiled in together with the hops and any other flavourings or adjuncts that are being added at that stage.

brewpub: A pub or restaurant that makes its own beer on the same site, like a modern-day alehouse, although some production can also take place off site. Examples in Ireland include the Franciscan Well in Cork, the Roadside Tavern in Lisdoonvarna, Co. Clare and the Donegal Brewing Company at Dicey Reilly's.

brewster: A female brewer. See also pages 38–39.

CAMRA: In their own words, 'the Campaign for Real Ale is an independent, voluntary organisation campaigning for real ale, community pubs and consumer rights'. Founded in 1971 and based in St Albans, England, there are now over 200 branches throughout the UK, including Northern Ireland (see page 198), with over 158,000 members worldwide. See also *real ale*.

carbonation: The bubbles in beer, produced by carbon dioxide (CO_2). Carbonation is what gives a beer its 'scrubbing bubbles' property that refreshes your palate when drinking beer with a meal.

cask ale: Unfiltered, unpasteurised ale (also known as 'cask-conditioned ale' or 'real ale') that is stored, conditioned in and served from a cask. Cask ales are naturally carbonated, which means that no additional carbon dioxide or nitrogen are added. Cask ales are a live product that finish their conditioning in the pub, which is why a pub that takes good care of its cask ales is a place to be treasured. See also *real ale*.

cicerone: *Cicerone* is an old term for an expert guide, but in this context it means a beer sommelier – a certified beer expert who is knowledgeable about all aspects of beer, from its history and the many styles of beer to glassware and beer and food matching. The term is derived from the name of the Roman orator Cicero, who was famed for his formidable eloquence and learning.

conditioning: *Ageing* and *maturing* are synonymous terms for conditioning, which refers to the time needed for a beer to become the best version of itself. Conditioning includes bottle conditioning, cask conditioning and lagering.

contract brewing: When a business hires another brewery to actually make its beer but still controls its own recipes, sales, marketing, distribution, etc. In Ireland this is sometimes done until the business can get up and running in a brewery of its own.

cool-fermenting: See *bottom-fermenting*.

copper: See *brew kettle*.

craft beer: Although the term is not strictly defined or regulated, craft beer is generally taken to mean high-quality beer produced in small batches by an independent craft brewery. See pages 32–34 for a more in-depth discussion.

craft brewery: Often used interchangeably with the term *microbrewery*, although *craft brewery* and *craft beer* are the preferred terms these days, as they denote the beer's artisan pedigree, even when a microbrewery evolves and expands beyond its small-scale beginnings. See also *microbrewery*.

draught beer: Beer served from a cask or keg rather than from a bottle. This is the beer that is on tap at the pub.

dry hopping: Adding hops to the beer at a low temperature towards the end of fermentation, when the hops are left to infuse the beer for a few days or up to several weeks. This technique boosts hop aroma and flavour without the bitterness that is drawn out by heat.

EBU: European bitterness units. See *IBU.*

esters: A chemical compound formed by yeast during fermentation, esters are responsible for fruity or floral flavours and aromas. Or if you have ever thought a beer tasted or smelled like nail polish remover, that was the esters talking. Since esters are formed more readily during warm fermentation, ales have more estery characteristics than lagers.

ethanol: The alcohol in beer, which is produced by yeast. It is not only intoxicating, but can have a warming, drying or astringent effect on your palate too. ABV measures the amount of ethanol in beer.

fermentation: This is where the magic happens – fermentation occurs when the yeast is added to the boiled, cooled wort, transforming the sugar to alcohol and carbon dioxide. It takes two to three weeks for ales and up to six weeks or more for lagers to fully ferment. There are three types of fermentation: cool (bottom), warm (top) and wild.

finish: See *aftertaste*.

gastropub: A mash-up of the words 'gastronomy' and 'pub', gastropubs were a late-twentieth-century invention as pubs sought to reinvent themselves by serving good food in addition to beer. Gastropubs started in the UK, but they have spread to Ireland now too. See page 142–145 for a listing of some of the top gastropubs around Ireland.

gravity: The density of the wort, which is measured at two distinct stages. Original gravity measures the density of the wort compared to water before the beer starts fermenting; it measures how much sugar is in the wort and is a good indicator of how alcoholic the final beer will be. Final gravity is the density measurement after the beer has finished fermenting. The alcoholic strength of the beer can be calculated by finding the difference between the original gravity and the final gravity.

growler: A large glass or ceramic jug that you take to the pub for them to fill up with draught or cask beer so that you can take it home.

gruit: A mixture of herbs and spices that was used to flavour beer before hops were in widespread use. Commonly used herbs included bog myrtle, yarrow, wild rosemary, heather, juniper, ginger, caraway and cinnamon.

gypsy brewing: Gypsy brewers are nomads with no fixed abode. They collaborate with existing breweries, using their equipment to create special one-off beers, and then they move on.

head: The frothy or creamy foam that sits on top of a beer, ranging in colour from snow white to a latte shade of brown. See also page 57.

hops: The female flowers of the hop plant (*Humulus lupulus*), which give beer its bitterness and piney, citrusy flavours and aromas. Hops help to preserve the beer too. See also pages 11–16.

IBU: International bitterness units, a scale that measures the bitterness of beer. In general, a beer with a low IBU will taste less bitter than a beer with a high IBU. See also page 16.

keeving: A centuries-old way of making naturally sweet, sparkling cider by carefully controlling the fermentation. The process is still used in France and the UK.

lacing: The foam that clings to a beer glass after you take a sip.

lauter tun: The vessel in which the sweet wort is separated from the mash by allowing the liquid to drain away through thin slits in the bottom that act as a sieve. The mash is then sparged in the lauter tun to extract most of the sugar from the grain.

lautering: The process in brewing whereby the mash is separated from the sweet wort in the mash tun or lauter tun. There are three steps in lautering: mashout, recirculation and sparging.

light strike: When ultraviolet light reacts with hop compounds, it produces catty or skunky flavours or aromas. Beware of beer in clear or green bottles, as this will likely be a problem.

macrobrewery: Another term for the big brands that mass-produce beer. You know who they are.

malt: The brewing process begins with malt, which is cereal grains (usually barley) that are soaked in water to make them germinate, then heated and dried (malted) in order to halt the enzymes and develop the desired characteristics, from the bready, biscuity flavours of pale malts to the chocolate or roasted coffee flavours of dark malts. See also pages 7–11.

mash: When the milled barley (or other grain) is mixed with hot water in the mash tun and left to steep, the resulting porridgey goop is called mash.

mash tun: The vat in which the milled barley (or other grain) is steeped in hot water in order to extract the sugars.

mashing: Like the tea-making stage of brewing, mashing is the process of steeping milled malted barley (or other grain) in hot water in order to convert the grain's starch to sugar and kick off the brewing process. The resulting liquid is called wort.

microbrewery: A small-scale brewery producing high-quality beer. In Ireland, microbreweries produce less than 20,000hl (2 million litres) per year, as that is the limit for availing of favourable tax rates. (For comparison's sake, Guinness brews 1.75 million litres of beer every *day* in Dublin.) See also *craft brewery*.

mouthfeel: The sum total of a beer's body, texture, carbonation and flavour and how it all feels on your palate. See also *astringent* and *body* and page 53.

nanobrewery: Called 'the garage bands of the craft beer world' by *The New York Times*, nanos are one step up from a home brewer. In the US, the definition of a nanobrewery is one that has a brew system that is four US barrels (470 litres) or less, but is still fully regulated and licensed. Nanos are often a stepping stone on the way to becoming a fully fledged microbrewery.

noble hops: European hop varieties with high aroma and low bitterness.

nucleated: Nucleated beer glasses have etchings and pits in the bottom of the glass that help to release the gas in the beer and therefore keep up a steady stream of bubbles and preserve the head. Without it, the head of a beer can quickly go flat.

oxidation: If beer and oxygen get together while the beer is ageing, the beer can develop stale flavours and aromas reminiscent of wet cardboard or sherry.

pasteurisation: Regarded as the father of modern brewing, in the 1870s, Louis Pasteur discovered that by heating beer, wine and milk and then cooling it quickly, bacteria could be killed, thus sterilising and stabilising the beer (or wine or milk) and preventing it from spoiling. This process became known as pasteurisation. Pasteurisation is good for extending shelf life (and thus shipping beer), but can be bad for flavour and freshness. Cask ales and bottle-conditioned beers are unpasteurised, and thus are still a living product.

phenolic: Medicinal, tarry, carbolic, spicy, smoky or clove-like flavours or aromas in beer. This is acceptable in some styles (like the signature clove aroma and flavour in a wheat beer), but it is usually a flaw.

pomace: The dry pulp that is left after all the juice has been pressed out of the apples when making cider.

racking: Drawing the beer off the spent yeast sediment and transferring it to another vessel.

real ale: CAMRA coined the term 'real ale' in the 1970s in the UK. They define it as 'a beer brewed from traditional ingredients (malted barley, hops, water and yeast), matured by secondary fermentation in the container from which it is dispensed, and served without the use of extraneous carbon dioxide. [...] It is literally living as it continues to ferment in the cask in your local pub, developing its flavour as it matures, ready to be poured into your glass. Real ale is also known as "cask-conditioned beer", "real cask ale", "real beer" and "naturally conditioned beer".' Though generally assumed to mean beer served from a cask, real ale covers bottle-conditioned beers too. See also *bottle-conditioned*, *CAMRA* and *cask ale*.

Saccharomyces cerevisiae: A top-fermenting yeast used when brewing ales. It is also used in the production of bread, cheese, wine and distilling spirits, making it one hardworking little strain. Small but mighty? You bet. See also *top-fermenting*.

Saccharomyces pastorianus: A bottom-fermenting yeast used when brewing lagers. This strain of yeast is named after Louis Pasteur, who figured out how to stop micro-organisms from spoiling beer and made modern brewing possible. See also *bottom-fermenting*.

secondary fermentation: A type of ageing or conditioning that takes place in a fresh container away from the sediment that settled to the bottom of the first fermentation tank. It can take anywhere from several days to months. Bottle-conditioned beer and cask ales undergo a secondary fermentation in their respective containers.

session beer: A low-alcohol (usually 3–5% ABV), well-balanced, nicely drinkable beer – the kind that you would be happy to knock back over the course of a night out, when you are likely to be having a few pints but don't want to lose the run of yourself or suffer unduly for it in the morning.

skunked: See *light strike*.

sparging: The step in lautering where hot water is gently sprinkled through the grain to extract every last bit of sugar (the word 'sparge' means 'to spray or sprinkle'). To help you visualise it, some home brewers use a watering can for this step. The water cannot be the wrong temperature or the wrong pH – it has to be just right in order to avoid releasing unwanted tannins into the wort. See also *lautering*.

spent grains: A by-product of the mashing process, after which point the grain has given up most of its sugars to the beer, but still has some protein and fibre left. See also page 21.

terroir: Loosely translated as 'a sense of place' (the French word means 'local'). See also page 33.

top-fermenting: Ale yeasts that ferment rapidly at warm temperatures (between 10°C and 25°C), producing complex fruity and spicy flavours and aromas. The yeast rises to the top of the fermentation vessel, creating a rich, thick yeast head.

volatiles: The things that give beer its aroma when they evaporate, such as hop oils, esters, spices and even the alcohol itself. The head on a beer catches delicate volatiles in its net of bubbles, which is one of the reasons why a good head is an important component of a beer overall. Using the right glassware helps head development and retention, and hence boosts the impact of the volatiles.

warm-fermenting: See *top-fermenting*.

wet-hopped: Beer made with fresh hops straight off the bine, as opposed to the more common dried hop pellets. As such, these are seasonal beers and are only available where hops are grown. Also known as *fresh hop beer* or *fresh hop ale*.

widget: Patented by Guinness in the 1980s, a widget is about the size of a table tennis ball (a rocket-shaped widget is used for bottles) and is inserted into cans or bottles, usually of stout. When the can or bottle is opened, the widget creates a smooth, creamy head, similar to beer served on draught, due to the nitrogen in it being released.

wort: When the malted barley (or other grain) is steeped in hot water in the mash tun, the resulting sugar-rich amber liquid is wort. It is called sweet wort before the hops are added, then hopped wort after it is transferred to the brew kettle and boiled with the hops.

yeast: The microbe magicians that turn sugar into alcohol and carbon dioxide. Beer is divided into one of two major categories according to which type of yeast is used: ale yeast or lager yeast. Ale yeasts are used for top-fermenting beers, while lager yeasts are used for bottom-fermenting beers.

zymology: The art or chemistry of fermentation processes, as in brewing beer, making wine, distilling and other fermented foods and drinks. Zymology is also known as zymurgy, which is often the last word in the dictionary, though it is sometimes pipped at the post by zythum, which fittingly enough is an ancient drink made from fermented malt. A handy word to have up your sleeve for Scrabble.

BIBLIOGRAPHY

Allen, D., *Irish Traditional Cooking: Over 300 Recipes from Ireland's Heritage*. Dublin: Gill & Macmillan, 2012.

Allen, D., *The Forgotten Skills of Cooking: The Time-Honoured Ways Are the Best – Over 700 Recipes Show You Why*. London: Kyle Cathie, 2009.

Anderson, G. and McLaughlin, J., *Farmhouse Cheese of Ireland: A Celebration*. Wilton, Co. Cork: The Collins Press, 2011.

Andrews, C., *The Country Cooking of Ireland*. San Francisco: Chronicle Books, 2009.

Beckett, F. and Beckett, W., *An Appetite for Ale*. St Albans: CAMRA Books, 2007.

Bernstein, J.M., *Brewed Awakening: Behind the Beers and Brewers Leading the World's Craft Brewing Revolution*. New York: Sterling Epicure, 2011.

Bernstein, J.M., *The Complete Beer Course. Boot Camp for Beer Geeks: From Novice to Expert in Twelve Tasting Classes*. New York: Sterling Epicure, 2013.

Boteler, A., *The Gourmet's Guide to Cooking with Beer*. Beverly, MA: Quarry Books, 2009.

Brennan, M., 'Drinkers on duty as microbrewers enjoy excise cut', *Irish Independent*, 24 November 2012.

Brown, P., *Man Walks into a Pub: A Sociable History of Beer*. London: Pan Macmillan, 2010.

Brown, P. and Bradshaw, B., *World's Best Cider*. London: Jacqui Small, 2013.

Burn-Callander, R., 'A craft beer revolution is brewing', *Telegraph*, 13 December 2013.

Campbell, G., *Georgina Campbell's Ireland: The Best of Irish Food and Hospitality*, 12th edition. Dublin: Epicure Press, 2013.

Carrigy, A., 'There's eating and drinking in them', *The Irish Times*, 26 March 2014.

Cassidy, M., 'Armagh Bramley growers celebrate special EU status', BBC, 8 March 2012.

Clancy, T., 'Cider house rules', *Sunday Business Post*, 16 September 2012.

Cole, M., *Let Me Tell You About Beer: A Beginner's Guide to All Things Brewed*. London: Pavilion Books, 2011.

Dermody, J., 'Brewers stress €1.2bn contribution to the economy and call for excise cut', *Irish Examiner*, 22 February 2014.

Dodd, J., *The Craft Beer Cookbook*. Avon, MA: Adams Media, 2013.

Dromey, T., 'Cider-maker presses ahead with plans for expansion', *Irish Examiner*, 19 August 2013.

Ernst & Young, *The Contribution Made by Beer to the European Economy*. Amsterdam, December 2013.

European Beer Consumers Union (EBCU), *Manifesto*. St Albans, 2013.

Evans, J., *CAMRA's Book of Beer Knowledge: Essential Wisdom for the Discerning Drinker*. St Albans: CAMRA Books, 2011.

Farley, D., 'Dining in Dublin, from boxty to blaa', *The New York Times*, 29 January 2014.

Fennell, J. and Bunbury, T., *The Irish Pub*. London: Thames & Hudson, 2008.

Fisher, C., 'It's not small beer: Big profits being made from tiny labels', *Irish Independent*, 26 January 2014.

Fletcher, J., *Cheese & Beer*. Kansas City, MO: Andrews McMeel Publishing, 2013.

Griffiths, I., *Beer and Cider in Ireland: The Complete Guide*. Dublin: Liberties Press, 2007.

Hartley, P., *Guinness: An Official Celebration of 250 Remarkable Years*. London: Hamlyn, 2009.

Healy, A., 'Pubs need to "change approach"', *The Irish Times*, 25 January 2012.

Hennerty, M., *The Heritage Apples of Ireland*. Dublin: Department of Agriculture, Food and the Marine, 2014.

Hogg, R., *The British Pomology: The History, Description, Classification, and Synonymes, of the Fruits and Fruit Trees of Great Britain*. Cambridge: Cambridge University Press, 2012 (first published 1851).

Hornsey, I.S., *A History of Beer and Brewing*. Cambridge: Royal Society of Chemistry Publishing, 2003.

Hospitality Ireland, 'Molson Coors buys craft beer brand Franciscan Well', 15 January 2013.

Hughes, D., *A Bottle of Guinness Please: The Colourful History of Guinness*. Phimboy, 2006.

Hyland, P., '(Micro)brewing up a storm: How Ireland's craft beers are making their mark', *TheJournal.ie*, 29 July 2013.

Ireland, Revenue – Irish Tax & Customs, *PN 1888 – Repayment of Alcohol Products Tax on Beer Produced in Qualifying Microbreweries*, October 2013.

Irish Independent, 'Demise of crab apple leaves a sour taste', 24 November 2012.

Keane, J., 'Limerick Breweries', *The Old Limerick Journal*, Vol. 8, autumn 1981, pp. 17–20.

Kelly, F., 'Trees in early Ireland', *Irish Forestry: Journal of the Society of Irish Foresters*, Vol. 56, No. 1, 1999, pp. 39–57.

Koch, G. and Wagner, S., *The Craft of Stone Brewing Co*. Berkeley, CA: Ten Speed Press, 2011.

Lamb, J.G. and Hayes, A., *The Irish Apple: History and Myth*. Scariff, Co. Clare: Irish Seed Savers Association, 2012.

Lecky, W.E.H., 'Ireland: 1700–1760' in *A History of England in the Eighteenth Century*, Vol. 2. London: Longmans, Green & Co., 1878, 1917.

Lennon, B.W. and Doyle, E., *Wild Food. Nature's Harvest: How to Gather, Cook and Preserve*. Dublin: O'Brien Press, 2013.

Lewis, S., *A Topographical Dictionary of Ireland*, Vol. 2. London: S. Lewis & Co., 1849.

Lynch, P. and Vaizey, J., *Guinness's Brewery in the Irish Economy 1759–1876*. Cambridge: Cambridge University Press, 1960.

Lyons, P., 'Beer could be the answer to all our economic woes', *Irish Independent*, 7 July 2013.

Mahon, B., *Land of Milk and Honey: The Story of Traditional Irish Food and Drink*. Dublin: Poolbeg, 1991.

Mansfield, S., *The Search for God and Guinness: A Biography of the Beer that Changed the World*. Nashville, TN: Thomas Nelson, 2009.

Mathias, P., *The Brewing Industry in England, 1700–1830*. Cambridge: Cambridge University Press, 1959.

McGreevy, R., 'Changing tastes: The rise and rise of craft beers', *The Irish Times*, 3 February 2014.

McKenna, J. and McKenna, S., *The Irish Food Guide*, 10th edition. Durrus, Co. Cork: Estragon Press, 2012.

McKenna, S., *Extreme Greens: Understanding Seaweeds*. Durrus, Co. Cork: Estragon Press, 2013.

Mercurio, P., *Cooking with Beer*. Millers Point, NSW: Murdoch Books Australia, 2011.

Mulvihill, M., *Ingenious Ireland: A County-by-County Exploration of Irish Mysteries and Marvels*. Dublin: TownHouse & CountryHouse Ltd, 2002.

Nelis, G., 'Craft brewing bubbles up', *Sunday Business Post*, 28 July 2013.

O'Rourke, T., 'Brewing Glossary'. London: The Institute of Brewing and Distilling, 2008.

O'Rourke, T., *The Good Craft Brewery Guide to Ireland*. Self-published, 2013.

Oliver, G. (ed.), *The Oxford Companion to Beer*. New York: Oxford University Press, 2012.

Oliver, G., *The Brewmaster's Table: Discovering the Pleasures of Real Beer with Real Food*. New York: Ecco, 2003.

Osborne, H., 'Matching food and cider', *Guardian*, 11 August 2009.

Pearson, L., *The Brewing Industry: A Report by the Brewery History Society for English Heritage*. Longfield, Kent: Brewery History Society, February 2010.

Percival, G., 'Global sales of Guinness fall as Irish and Nigerian beer markets decline', *Irish Examiner*, 31 January 2014.

Perozzi, C. and Beaune, H., *The Naked Pint: An Unadulterated Guide to Craft Beer*. New York: Perigee, 2009.

Pollan, M., *Cooked: A Natural History of Transformation*. London: Allen Lane, 2013.

Portadown Times, 'Town apple growing family are hoping for slice of drink market', 1 May 2014.

Protz, R., 'Rise of the microbrewery: Small but perfectly formed', *Independent*, 27 March 2010.

Riegal, R., 'Crafty devils brew up a storm in beer industry', *Irish Independent*, 16 September 2013.

Robins, N., *Apron Strings*. Dublin: New Island, 2013.

Rotunno, T., 'More pour into craft beer market, but it's not a bubble', CNBC, 19 October 2013.

Rowe, P., 'Heady prediction: Craft beer sales to double by 2020', *U-T San Diego*, 5 December 2013.

Saunders, L., *Cooking with Beer*. Alexandria, VA: Time Life Books, 1996.

Saunders, L., *The Best of American Beer and Food: Pairing and Cooking with Craft Beer*. Boulder, CO: Brewers Publications, 2007.

Schaap, R., 'A drinker's guide to Dublin', *The New York Times*, 7 June 2012.

Schultz, S., *Beer, Food, and Flavor: A Guide to Tasting, Pairing, and the Culture of Craft Beer*. New York: Skyhorse Publishing, 2012.

Sexton, R., *A Little History of Irish Food*. London: Kyle Cathie, 1998.

Sheehan, A., 'Beer sales fall flat as drinkers abandon pubs', *Irish Independent*, 22 October 2012.

Smith, C., *The Ancient and Present State of the County and City of Cork: Containing a Natural, Civil, Ecclesiastical, Historical and Topographical Description Thereof*, Vol. 1. Cork: John Connor, 1815.

Smithers, R., 'Pubs boosted by 197 new breweries opening in Britain in last year', *Guardian*, 12 September 2013.

Tepedelen, A., *The Brewtal Truth Guide to Extreme Beers*. Guilford, CT: Lyons Press, 2013.

The Farmer's Magazine, 'Cider and perry', Vol. 23, 1863, p. 530.

Twomey, C., 'Raise a glass to the craft brewer', *Galway Independent*, 2 October 2013.

Tyack, K.R., *Wild Kitchens*. Auckland: HarperCollins, 2012.

Unger, R.W., *Beer in the Middle Ages and the Renaissance*. Philadelphia, PA: University of Pennsylvania Press, 2004.

Wakefield, E.G., *An Account of Ireland, Statistical and Political*, Vol. 1. London: Longman, Hurst, Rees, Orme & Brown, 1812.

Watson, B., *Cider Hard and Sweet: History, Traditions, and Making Your Own*, 3rd edition. Woodstock, VT: The Countryman Press, 2013.

Whelan, P. and McGuinness, K., *The Irish Beef Book*. Dublin: Gill & Macmillan, 2013.

Wilson, J., 'Apple of Armagh's eye', *The Irish Times*, 30 June 2012.

Winterman, D., 'Beer: The women taking over the world of brewing', *BBC News Magazine*, 23 January 2014.

Young, A., *A Tour in Ireland 1776–1779*. London: George Bell & Sons, 1892.

Zekaria, S., 'In Europe, a taste grows for craft beer', *Wall Street Journal*, 14 August 2012.

INDEX

ACKNOWLEDGEMENTS

It takes a village to write a book, but in this case it took an entire industry. Thank you to each and every one of the brewers and cider-makers who took time out of their busy days to talk to us. Without all your hard work, there would be no reason for this book to exist. A special thank you goes to Daniel Emerson from Stonewell Cider for fact checking and advice, as well as to Emma Tyrrell from Cider Ireland and Mark Jenkinson from The Cider Mill. Thank you to all at Eight Degrees Brewing, particularly Scott Baigent and Cam Wallace, who had to patiently endure Caroline's endless questions, many baking-with-beer experiments and ever-present camera.

Thank you to Eoin Purcell, editorial director at New Island, who believed in this book from the very beginning. Thank you to our eagle-eyed editor Justin Corfield, whose spot-on suggestions and selfless research in verifying some of our suggested beer and food pairings made this a better book. Our typesetter, Mariel Deegan, incorporated all our ideas with the good-natured patience of a saint – the next round's on us, Mariel! And last but not least, thank you to Erik Johansson from The Green Man Studio, who made the vision we had for the cover and the illustrations a reality that is even better than what we could have imagined.

Thank you to our agent, Sharon Bowers, who always says just the right thing at just the right time to keep two nervous new authors on track. And a special thank you to Imen McDonnell, who introduced us to Sharon in the first place.

Thank you to Darina Allen for making time in her whirlwind schedule at the Ballymaloe Cookery School to write the foreword. Thank yous are also in order for Georgina Campbell and John McKenna – they were two of our first readers, and as food writers for whom we have the very highest respect and admiration, their praise for the book means more than we can say.

Big thank yous also go to Seáneen Sullivan from L. Mulligan Grocer and Kevin Sheridan from Sheridans Cheesemongers for sharing their tips on matching beer and cider with food and cheese – we are all the lucky beneficiaries of their hard-won wisdom.

Acknowledgements

Thank you to John Duffy and Reuben Gray of Beoir, Carley Donegan, Bruce Mansour and Seamus O'Hara of the Irish Craft Beer and Cider Festival, the Malting Company of Ireland, New Zealand Hops for letting Caroline visit at the busiest time of the year and Waimea Hops owner George Hill.

Thank you to Derry Clarke, Sarah Galvin, Lilly Higgins, Michael Hunter, Imen McDonnell, Katy McGuinness, Sally McKenna, Jess Murphy, Lily Ramirez-Foran, Sarah Roarty, Nessa Robins, Donal Skehan and Pat Whelan for sharing your recipes – it was delicious work to test them all.

Thank you to Bord Bia, Carlow Brewing Company, Dovehill Orchard, Dungarvan Brewing Company, Galway Bay Brewery, Lilly Higgins, Longueville House, Mac Ivors, Imen McDonnell, Olan McNeece (Dan Kelly's Cider), Declan Moore, Seán O'Reilly (Toasty Oak), Lily Ramirez-Foran, Kevin Sheridan, Donal Skehan, Seáneen Sullivan and J.W. Sweetman for so generously sharing your photos.

Thanks, too, to all the Irish beer and food bloggers for championing Irish producers, and without whom the internet would be a far less fascinating and friendly place. We count ourselves lucky indeed that our tentative tweets and online comments in the early days of the Irish food blogging scene have turned into lasting friendships in the real world.

It's not easy being a brewer by day and a muse and fount of brewing knowledge by night, but Caroline has to thank Scott for bearing it all with good grace, trying every experimental dish (that spiced buttered beer was definitely a non-runner!) that emerged from the kitchen and for sharing his craft beer dream with her.

Kristin thanks Matt, maker of countless cups of coffee, minder of children, runner of errands, reader of drafts, organiser of couriers and all-round helper and husband extraordinaire while she wrote this book, and always.

And of course thank you to all of you, the readers and drinkers who are fuelling the craft drinks revolution. *Sláinte*!

Journalist and broadcaster CAROLINE HENNESSY developed an interest in and appreciation for craft beer while living in New Zealand. One of Ireland's first food bloggers, she started the award-winning www.bibliocook.com in 2005. Together with Kristin Jensen she set up the Irish Food Bloggers' Association in 2010. She writes for the McKennas' Good Food Guides, is a member of the Irish Food Writers' Guild and is devoted to exploring the intersecting worlds of Irish craft beer and fine Irish food. She lives in North Cork with her brewer husband and two small girls who want to be brewers when they grow up.

KRISTIN JENSEN is a freelance editor specialising in cookery books and has worked with many of Ireland's top food writers and chefs. She explores Ireland with an appetite, blogs at Edible Ireland and is a member of the Irish Food Writers' Guild. Originally from the US, she moved to Ireland in 1999 and now lives in the countryside in County Louth with her husband and two children.